100 IDEAS
FOR SECONDARY SCHOOL
ASSEMBLIES

CONTINUUM ONE HUNDREDS SERIES

100 IDEAS
FOR
SECONDARY
SCHOOL
ASSEMBLIES

Susan Elkin

continuum

Continuum International Publishing Group
The Tower Building   80 Maiden Lane, Suite 704
11 York Road   New York, NY 10038
SE1 7NX

www.continuumbooks.com

British Library Cataloguing-in-Publication Data
A catalogue record for this book is available from the British Library.

ISBN: 0826493971 (paperback)

Library of Congress Cataloging-in-Publication Data
Elkin, Susan.
    100 ideas for assemblies : secondary school edition / Susan Elkin.
        p. cm. -- (Continuum one hundreds series)
    ISBN-13: 978-0-8264-9397-2 (pbk.)
    ISBN-10: 0-8264-9397-1 (pbk.)
    1.   Schools--Exercises and recreations. 2.   Student activities.   I. Title. II. Title: One hundred ideas for assemblies. III. Title: Hundred ideas for assemblies. IV. Series.

  LB3015.E55 2007
  373.18'95--dc22

2006029551

Typeset by Ben Cracknell Studios | www.benstudios.co.uk
Printed and bound in Great Britain by Ashford Colour Press, Gosport, Hampshire

CONTENTS

SECTION 2 **A focus on behaviour**

SECTION 3 Topical issues

SECTION 4 Using music, art and literature

SECTION 5 **Single class assemblies**

SECTION 6 **Class-led assemblies**

SECTION 7 **Instant fixes**

A secondary school assembly is not a lesson. It's a gathering of students and staff, usually from different classes or year groups, to share experiences, information, thoughts, viewpoints, codes, cultures, beliefs and ideas which might relate to the curriculum, but which are not directly part of it.

The assembly was born as the 'daily act of collective worship', which became a compulsory part of state school life after the 1944 Education Act. But the day of the reading-hymn-prayer assembly has long gone in most schools, although many faith schools still conduct what is effectively a mini-service each day. Usually 'collective worship' is now a very loose and wide-ranging concept, partly because a daily Christian service is inappropriate in schools with a large multi-faith population, but also because far fewer teachers feel comfortable leading a Christian mini-service than used to.

So what we're usually left with is the catch-all assembly. By law it is supposed to happen every day somewhere in the school. However, a secondary school hall which accommodates the whole school is a rarity in the twenty-first century. So, in practice, it is a cross-section of the school that assembles, which means that most students attend assembly only on certain days of the week. Some schools also have a system of class assemblies, typically taken by the form tutor or teacher in the tutor room.

Assemblies are fun and a good opportunity for creativity – both yours and that of any students you involve. They are very useful mop-up occasions when you can, with impunity, visit topics which don't quite fit anywhere else. Think cross-curricular and think extra-curricular. Stray into RE, English, history, geography, citizenship, PSHE, music and almost anywhere else you wish.

A good assembly needs some sort of 'spiritual' dimension so that it isn't just a large-scale lesson. Many of the suggestions and ideas in this book have a religious basis, or can be easily be given one if appropriate, but often a few seconds' silence to think about an issue, or finishing with a thoughtful poem or piece of music is all it takes to give an assembly the right flavour. The aim should always be for students (and staff colleagues) to leave the assembly thinking about something in a new way.

Some assemblies are taken by headteachers and/or their deputies and can help them to build a relationship with pupils they don't teach. Others are taken by teachers, often on a rota. Assembly-leading is a good learning experience. Teachers develop both through doing it and from observing colleagues in action.

The 100 ideas in this book are starting points for anyone who has to take a secondary school assembly – they are all adaptable. Think of them as basic recipes, then add your own spices, herbs and favourite ingredients. In general, your own anecdotes – about *your* dog or *your* first car, for example – will work better with your students than anything you've taken from a book, so feel free to mix and match.

No apologies, by the way, for suggesting mostly music (and poems) which will be new to the majority of students. If you stick to what they are already familiar with you are missing a horizon-widening opportunity. Education is about discovery. New material in assemblies can be part of that.

Make the most of assemblies. They're one of the few opportunities in secondary school life to teach and learn off-piste. Enjoy them.

Special days

These ideas are in approximate date order as they occur through the year, although some do not have fixed dates.

TWELFTH NIGHT

This is for 6 January, which used to be Christmas Day. The old calendar was changed in the sixteenth century and new arrangements made including leap years because it was nearly two weeks out. But churches in the East – in Russia, for example – still celebrate Christmas on 6 January.

For many years, Christmas in Britain has traditionally lasted 12 days. The weather is cold and short days meant that farm workers years ago couldn't do much outdoor work, so they could have a long rest. 6 January is also celebrated by Christians in Europe and America as the Epiphany – the day when the wise men visited the baby Jesus in the stable (the word 'epiphany' is from Greek and means a moment of supernatural revelation).

Shakespeare's play *Twelfth Night* is about people falling in love and playing tricks on each other. Twelfth Night used to be regarded as a time for a party.

For your assembly, explain the significance of 6 January. Can you get a student, group of students or even the whole assembly to sing 'The Twelve Days of Christmas'? If you have video/DVD/electronic whiteboard facility in the hall you could show a short clip from one of the film versions of *Twelfth Night* or read aloud T. S. Eliot's poem 'Journey of the Magi'.

You will need:
o Notes on 6 January
o A DVD of *Twelfth Night* or copy of the poem 'Journey of the Magi'
o The words of 'The Twelve Days of Christmas'.

This is for 27 January or a day close to it. In Germany and Poland between 1940 and 1945 more than six million people were killed by the Nazi party which was in power in Germany. Most of those who died were Jewish men, women and children, but disabled people, gypsies and others regarded as a nuisance were also sent to the gas chambers.

The word 'holocaust' comes originally from the Greek word for burning. It has come to mean great destruction or loss of life and is used as shorthand for the dreadful crimes committed in Nazi Germany in the 1940s.

Holocaust Memorial Day started in 2000. The idea is to ensure that the horrors and the deaths are not forgotten. The day is also used to mourn other genocides. Each year there is a specific theme and a different city acts as host, although there are activities all over the country. See www.hmd.org.uk for more information.

Build your assembly around 'man's inhumanity to man' (Robert Burns). Explain what 'genocide' is and what happened in Germany during World War Two and elsewhere since. Point out that remembering and being aware is an important part of trying to ensure that it doesn't happen again.

It would be highly appropriate to end with a minute's silence.

You will need:
o Notes on the Holocaust.

IDEA

3

ACCESSION OF QUEEN ELIZABETH II

This is for 6 February or a day close to it. Queen Elizabeth II was born in 1926. She was Princess Elizabeth of York (like Princesses Beatrice and Eugenie today) and the granddaughter of King George V and Queen Mary.

Her father, King George VI, died of lung cancer on 6 February 1952. At the time the young Elizabeth, aged 25, was in Kenya with her husband. She had to fly straight home – wearing black for mourning – to be greeted as Britain's new Queen.

She has been Queen – Head of State – ever since. Queen Victoria reigned for 64 years, George III for 60, and Henry III for 56, so the Queen is working towards breaking records. In Britain the Head of State does not run the country. They appoint a Prime Minister and political party to do so once they've been elected by the people.

The Queen usually spends 6 February quietly at Sandringham in Norfolk. She won't celebrate the anniversary of her father's death, which she likes to remember in private.

Build an assembly around the Queen's accession, life and reign. Show a Jubilee mug or some other item commemorating the reign. Point out the significance of being an unelected Head of State. You might also mention the Queen's children and the line of succession.

You could play the National Anthem on CD or have it performed on piano or by an ensemble, and ask the students to stand, having explained why.

You will need:
o Notes on Queen Elizabeth II
o A recording or performance of the National Anthem
o A commemorative item, such as a Jubilee mug or plate.

The date of Chinese New Year varies, but it usually falls between mid-January and mid-February. Chinese people in China and all over the world – and there's a 'Chinatown' in most western cities – celebrate New Year on this day. It is also called spring festival or Lunar New Year. The date changes because it's linked with the phases of the moon.

Each New Year is associated with one of 12 animals. They are the Chinese signs of the Zodiac, rather like Aquarius, Capricorn and Gemini in the western world. 2007 is the year of the Pig (New Year falls on 18 February), 2008 is the Rat (7 February), 2009 is the Ox (26 January), 2010 is the Tiger (14 February), 2011 is the Rabbit (3 February), 2012 is the Dragon (23 January) and 2013 is the Snake (31 January).

Among Chinese people everywhere gifts, flowers and sweets are exchanged. Houses are cleaned and people visit temples. Shops and businesses are closed. There's a special family meal on New Year's Eve, with a big emphasis on getting rid of bad luck and seeing in good luck for the New Year. See www.new-year.co.uk/chinese for more information.

Describe Chinese New Year to the students or, if you have pupils in the school of Chinese origin, get a group of them to prepare a shared presentation about what they do at Chinese New Year and why. Chinese lanterns, paper dragons and so on add to the atmosphere in the hall. Play some Chinese music.

You will need:
o Notes on Chinese New Year
o Chinese paper lanterns and other decorations
o An organized presentation by Chinese students if possible
o Chinese music.

CHINESE NEW YEAR

Since 1818, 26 January has been a national holiday in Australia. The country used to be a British colony and is still part of the Commonwealth. The holiday is a reminder of the arrival of the first British settlers in 1788.

Australia, the world's largest island, is the land of . . . kangaroos, surfboards, koalas, beach barbecues, boomerangs, TV soaps, hats with corks, sunshine, sharks and coral reefs. It is also a producer of wonderful fruit, such as sultanas, and buildings such as Sydney Opera House. Australians everywhere – from Nicole Kidman to Shane Warne – will be thinking of their country on this day. It's the heart of their summer; their schools have been on holiday since the end of November and don't go back until next month.

Plan an assembly to celebrate all the great things about Australia. Show a picture of Sydney Opera House (either hold it up or use an electronic whiteboard). Use as many visual aids as possible to symbolize Australia. Tell any anecdote or make any point about Australia you want to share – you could highlight sport such as cricket or rugby perhaps, or you could mention aboriginal music and instruments such as the didgeridoo.

Play a recording of 'Waltzing Matilda', Australia's unofficial national anthem, or perhaps a group of students could play/sing it.

You will need:
o Notes on Australia
o Pictures of Australia and other things to hold up, such as a boomerang if you happen to have one!
o A recording of, or music for, 'Waltzing Matilda'.

St Apollonia's Day falls on 9 February. She was an elderly, third-century nun in Alexandria. Christians were being persecuted and Apollonia was hit on the jaw by soldiers so hard that her teeth fell out. Then they said they'd burn her alive unless she renounced her faith. She wouldn't, but she leapt onto the pyre of her own accord in defiance.

Apollonia is the patron saint of dentists and toothache sufferers. If you see a painting of her in an art gallery or church, her symbol is a tooth, so you know it's her. There's even a dentistry journal in America called *The Apollonian*. She is the bearer of the British Dental Association's Royal Coat of Arms.

Make an assembly about dentists, toothache and how lucky we are to have modern dentists, orthodontists and hygienists to help keep teeth healthy and give us good smiles. Read aloud – or get a pupil to – Pam Ayres's poem 'I Wish I'd Looked After Me Teeth'.

Finish with half a minute's silence to remember or think of anyone you know who has troublesome and painful teeth.

You will need:
o A copy of 'I Wish I'd Looked After Me Teeth'
o *The Wordsworth Dictionary of Saints* or *The Oxford Dictionary of Saints* so that you can flesh out the story. (You'll find plenty of other good saints' stories there too.)

ST VALENTINE'S DAY

This is for 14 February or a date close to it. No one really knows who Valentine was. There are two possibilities. He may have been a Roman priest who was murdered on a road around 350 AD. Or perhaps he was a bishop who lived 60 miles from Rome, but who was taken there and killed in about 273 AD. Neither story says much for Claudius and Placidus who were the respective emperors who gave orders for the deaths. There is more about this in *The Wordsworth Dictionary of Saints*.

Meanwhile it's a day for sending cards and telling people that you love them – secretly or openly. No one is sure either why Valentine, whoever he was, came to be associated with couples in love. St Valentine is also the patron saint of bee keepers!

Build an assembly around what happens on St Valentine's Day and why. If you make the point that you can be in love at any age you can listen together to 'When I'm 64' by the Beatles. Shakespeare's 'Sonnet 116' – one of the greatest love poems ever written in English – works well on St Valentine's Day and you could replay the Beatles number as background while students leave the hall.

You will need:
○ Notes on the two Valentines if you want to flesh out their stories
○ A recording of 'When I'm 64' (from the album: *Sergeant Pepper's Lonely Hearts Club Band*)
○ 'Sonnet 116'.

The day before Lent starts is Shrove Tuesday. It falls six-and-a-half weeks before Easter, usually in February.

Shrove Tuesday is 'Pancake day' because years ago country people knew they were going to make sacrifices, including going without meat and other rich food, for 40 days from the following day, Ash Wednesday. They needed to use up any butter or fat they had left and so the tradition of making pancakes began. The fast is partly to remind Christians that Jesus 'lived rough' in the wilderness for 40 days before he began preaching.

In many countries Shrove Tuesday is called Mardi Gras (Fat Tuesday). People celebrate and have parties, as well as eating rich or fatty food. There are carnivals this week all over Europe and in other places where Christianity is strong, such as South America. The most famous carnival is in Venice, where people wear masks and take part in elaborate processions.

The word 'carnival' comes from Latin and means 'farewell meat' because it marks the beginning of a fast. 'Shrove' means forgiveness. On this day Christians went to their priests to be shriven or cleared of their sins. Pancake races, such as the annual one at Olney in Buckinghamshire each Shrove Tuesday, are a centuries-old British tradition.

During the assembly, pretend to make a pancake. Have a basin, whisk, frying pan, milk, eggs and oil to hand, and mime making, frying and tossing your pancake. Then explain the significance of Shrove Tuesday, perhaps showing pictures of a Mardi Gras carnival. You could also get a pupil to research the annual race at Olney in Buckinghamshire and tell the assembly about it.

You will need:
o Props for the pancake mime
o A student with a prepared reading
o Carnival pictures (not essential).

World Book Day is usually the first Thursday in March, but check from year to year. Sponsored by the Booksellers Association, it is a nationwide celebration of the importance and pleasure of books and there are lots of events. See www.worldbookday.com for further details of events taking place.

Make an assembly by showing pupils the Authorized Version of the Bible (1611) and the Q'ran, probably the two most important books ever written because they have influenced so many people for so long. Say a bit about each of them.

The most important secular book ever published is probably Shakespeare's *Complete Works*. Show a copy and say a bit about it. Then show a copy of your own favourite book (pick something suitable, such as *The Wind in the Willows*, *Gone With The Wind*, *Rebecca*, *The Silver Sword*, *Watership Down*, *Winnie the Pooh*). Talk about your book for a few minutes and recommend it.

Have ten students primed to stand up one by one and say the title and author of a book they'd like to recommend on World Book Day – like a list.

You will need:
o A copy of the Bible and the Q'ran
o Shakespeare's *Complete Works*
o Your favourite book
o Ten students and their favourite books.

Make sure that the students' books and the name of the book you have recommended are displayed afterwards all over the school, and check that the school library has plenty of copies of these books. Set this up in advance.

On 17 March Irish people all over the world remember their patron saint, wear green and/or the sign of the shamrock and think of their home country.

Born around 389 AD, probably somewhere in England or Scotland, Patrick came from a Christian family. Aged 16 he was captured by a raiding party and spent six years in Antrim as a slave, looking after his master's cattle. Eventually he escaped and went first to Britain and later to France. He studied for the priesthood and in the end became Bishop of Ireland, appointed by Pope Celestine I. He was, effectively, a missionary and played a big part in the conversion of the Irish to Christianity. He died on 17 March in 461 AD.

Legend has it that he drove the snakes out of Ireland, which is why there are no native snakes there. He is also supposed to have explained the doctrine of the Trinity using a shamrock and that is why it became Ireland's national emblem.

Make an assembly based on the story of St Patrick. You could wear something green and explain why. Show the shamrock and mention a few other things associated with Ireland, such as Guinness, Connemara marble, Westlife or Terry Wogan.

Play some Irish music – perhaps traditional folk music by a group such as The Dubliners.

You will need:
o An item of green clothing
o Notes on St Patrick and Ireland
o A recording of Irish music.

ST PATRICK'S DAY

MOTHERING SUNDAY

This is for a day during the week preceding the fourth Sunday in Lent, Mothering Sunday. It falls in March or April, three weeks before Easter. Mothering Sunday is a British, Christian tradition. The Americans celebrate 'Mother's Day' later in the year. The two have got confused, so Mothering Sunday is often wrongly called Mother's Day.

Servants working in big houses were given Mothering Sunday as a holiday to visit their mothers. The cook in the big kitchen gave each girl/lad a simnel cake to take home as a gift. It was a rich, layered cake, sandwiched with marzipan. The young servants also took flowers home, hence the modern custom of flowers for mums on Mothering Sunday.

Build an assembly about mothers and what a lot they do for families. Draw points from students. Cooking, shopping, ferrying around, hugging, providing support and encouragement are likely to come up. Explain the origins of Mothering Sunday and show a simnel cake or a picture of one.

One mother in particular once got a very special present. Cosima Wagner was the wife of the German composer, Richard Wagner. In 1870 she gave birth to a son Siegfried, named after a character in one of Richard's operas. Soon after, on Christmas morning, she woke to music. Her husband had composed the *Siegfried Idyll* for her as a surprise present and arranged for 15 musicians outside her window to play it.

Play part of the *Siegfried Idyll* and/or use it as the students file out.

You will need:
○ Notes on Mothering Sunday
○ A recording of Richard Wagner's *Siegfried Idyll*
○ A simnel cake or picture of one.

PALM SUNDAY

Use this towards the end of the spring term, before the school breaks up for Easter. At Easter Christians remember the death of Jesus, crucified by the Romans while Pontius Pilate was the local governor. He was put to death on a Friday, now remembered as Good (godly) Friday. According to the four gospels, Matthew, Mark, Luke and John, Jesus rose from the dead on the third day, which is now remembered on Easter Sunday.

The Bible describes exactly what Jesus and his 12 disciples did for the complete week of his death and resurrection, known as Holy Week. On the previous Sunday he borrowed a donkey and rode into Jerusalem. The excited crowd welcomed him by throwing down palm leaves for him to walk on and this day is now remembered as Palm Sunday, falling exactly a week before Easter.

Base an assembly on the significance of Palm Sunday. Explain the background. Read aloud (or prepare a student to do so) St Mark 11.1–11 and G. K. Chesterton's poem 'The Donkey'.

Then play 'Hosanna' from the musical *Jesus Christ Superstar*.

You will need:
o Notes on Palm Sunday and Easter
o Prepared readings (Bible and poem)
o A recording of *Jesus Christ Superstar*.

IDEA 13

APRIL FOOLS' DAY

April Fools' Day on 1 April is an old custom and no one is sure how it started. It may date from the Romans. Newspapers have fun with it and most will have one joke story on the day – such as the one in *The Times* a few years ago which said that the round shape of the Millennium Dome was based on a rare spider's web, complete with trick picture.

In France an April fool is a poisson d'avril (April fish) and in Scotland a gowk (cuckoo). In India similar tricks are played at the Holi Festival on 31 March.

Start your assembly by telling a silly story in a deadpan manner. You could, for example, tell the pupils that in future they will all be required to carry a red spotted handkerchief as part of the uniform (show them one, tell them where they can buy it and how much it costs, why it's essential, etc.). Or tell them that the school's science department has discovered a new strain of bacterium with very special qualities. Use your imagination and let rip!

Reveal eventually that you are fooling them. Remind them that April fools' jokes are just that – they are never harmful or spiteful. Remind pupils that the joking stops at midday.

You will need:

- Your carefully thought-out hoax story and any props it requires.

This is an idea for a day during the week before the London Marathon – usually the third Sunday in April, but check from year to year.

A marathon is a race on foot. Competitors have to cover 42.195 kilometres (26 miles and 385 yards). There is a marathon running event in the Olympic Games held every four years in various cities across the world (Beijing in 2008 and London in 2012). It was also part of the original Olympic Games held in Athens by the Ancient Greeks more than 2,000 years ago.

The name comes from a specific incident. Once – in 490 BC – there was a very fit messenger who ran with news of an army's victory more than 20 miles to Athens from the town of Marathon.

Marathons are now often organized for charity, with the runners sponsored to complete the distance. The London Marathon is the most famous in Britain. It was started in 1981 by champion runner Chris Brasher who had seen marathons working well in New York and Boston. The route begins in Greenwich and finishes in the Mall near Buckingham Palace, having wound its 26+ miles around various parts of London, including a big loop round the Isle of Dogs. Over 40,000 people take part each year, with most participants training for months beforehand. You have to apply and not everyone is accepted, but very large sums of money are raised each year.

Explain the background to the London Marathon. If there happens to be a member of staff, a student or someone known to the school community taking part so much the better. Involve him or her and ask them to talk a bit about their training. You could use a running singlet (modelled by a student?) as a prop.

You will need:
o Notes on the London Marathon
o A running singlet.

THE LONDON MARATHON

IDEA

15

Here's one for 23 April. No one knows exactly when William Shakespeare, Britain's greatest playwright was born. The year was 1564. There was no legal requirement to register a birth, but his baptism in the parish church in Stratford-upon-Avon was recorded on Sunday 26 April. High infant mortality meant that babies were always baptized quickly in case they died, so he was almost certainly born during the previous week.

23 April is St George's Day. St George – a Roman soldier about whom we know very little apart from a legend about his having fought a dragon – is the patron saint of England. And Shakespeare is our national playwright, so it makes sense to treat 23 April as his birthday, especially as, by a strange coincidence 52 years later in 1616, 23 April was the day Shakespeare died.

Shakespeare wrote 36 plays. Have 36 students ready to stand up in turn to say the names of the plays like a list. Show a clip of *Henry V*, Act III, Scene i, from 'Once more unto the breach' to 'God for England, Harry and St George'. Explain that this was a rallying cry as Henry tried to encourage his tired men to fight bravely against the French at Harfleur in the early fifteenth century.

English composer William Walton wrote the music for Laurence Olivier's famous 1944 film of *Henry V*, now quite well known in a concert arrangement. Play part of it and/or use it as the students leave the hall.

You will need:
○ Notes on Shakespeare and St George
○ Students rehearsed to reel off the names of all Shakespeare's plays
○ *Henry V* video or DVD ready in the right place
○ A recording of *Henry V* suite by William Walton.

World Red Cross Day falls on 8 May. The Red Cross was founded as an international organisation in 1863 by Swiss businessman Henry Dunant who had been horrified by the large numbers of untended wounded at the Battle of Solferino in 1859. It was, and is, based in Geneva, which is why its symbol is based on the Swiss flag. The idea was to alleviate suffering caused by disaster or war anywhere in the world. The Red Cross doesn't take sides and its neutrality is widely respected.

Today, some non-Christian cultures are uncomfortable with the symbol of the Christian cross so there is now a Red Crescent movement as well. In June 2006 a third – non-religious – symbol was agreed. Called the Red Crystal, it shows the outline of a red square tipped onto one corner to resemble a diamond shape on a white background. The symbolism of red on white is important because it suggests shed blood.

Show pictures of the three symbols and explain the background of the Red Cross movements. Mention specific war zones and disaster areas where the Red Cross is currently active. Give examples of the sort of work it does, such as putting together boxes of essentials for individuals in stricken areas. What might be included?

End with a minute's silence to think of the victims of war, poverty and disaster and all the people in the world risking their lives for those who need help.

You will need:
o Notes on Red Cross, Crescent and Crystal
o Pictures of the three symbols (banners could be made in advance and displayed prominently in the hall).

WORLD RED CROSS DAY

17

MIDSUMMER

This would work on 21 June (the longest day) or 24 June (Midsummer's Day) or on either of the dates between them. In the UK at this time of year it gets dark between 9.30 pm and 11 pm, depending how far south or north you are. It's the longest day and the shortest night.

Long before people had telescopes and understood how the Earth moves round the sun at an angle and varying distance to create seasons and days and nights of changing length, men (and women) noticed that the hours of daylight seemed to move. They often celebrated both the longest and shortest days. Stonehenge, for example, is built to catch the exact line of the sun on midsummer morning and must have had a religious significance. As someone once said, 'It's actually a calendar, but a bit big to hang on the wall!'

Parties are traditional at midsummer too. If it's fine that evening, or at the following weekend, there will be plenty of barbecues, concerts, performances, fireworks and so on. Shakespeare wrote a play called *A Midsummer Night's Dream* about a group of people dreaming about getting lost in a wood where strange things happen at midsummer.

Explain what midsummer is and why it is significant. Mention 'midsummer madness' and Shakespeare's play. Read aloud Shakespeare's summer love sonnet, number 18, 'Shall I compare thee to a summer's day?' Have six students ready with a sentence each on what they like most about midsummer.

Listen to 'Oh What a Beautiful Morning' from *Oklahoma* and then use it as play-out music.

You will need:
- Notes on midsummer
- A copy of 'Sonnet 18'
- Six students ready to state their favourite midsummer things
- A recording of *Oklahoma*.

4 July is Independence Day. Americans celebrate independence from Britain which they achieved in 1763, after what the British call The American War of Independence or 'losing the American colonies' and the Americans call The American Revolution, which neatly illustrates the big difference that a point of view can make.

It's a holiday in the USA and all Americans focus on their national identity. They decorate their homes elaborately with red, white and blue and variations of the American flag.

Have the hall decorated with American flags, perhaps made by students. Play a recording of 'The Stars and Stripes Forever'. Explain that many American school students have to reaffirm their allegiance to the USA every morning by formally saluting the flag in their classes. Then brainstorm things which we connect with America. You can either do this yourself, or have students primed to add items, or simply question the audience for spontaneous ideas. Avoid politics and conflicts, as this should be a cheerful and positive assembly. Things which you might want to mention include Hollywood, Mickey Mouse, chewing gum, McDonald's, cowboys, chipmunks, baseball, peanuts, Ford cars, drive-ins – compile your own list. As each thing is mentioned say a bit about it. If there are any Americans on the staff or among the students you could involve them too. Play out to 'The Stars and Stripes Forever'.

You will need:
○ Flags for the hall
○ Notes on the events of the 1760s if you want to cover the history of American Independence
○ A list of things connected with America
○ A recording of 'The Stars and Stripes Forever'.

This is an assembly to mark the start of Ramadan, the variable date when Muslims begin their annual fast. On this day (or this week) adult Muslims all over the world start a month-long fast, going without food, drink, smoking and sex during the hours of daylight. Of the five pillars of Islam – things that believers think are crucial – fasting, or 'sawm', is the fourth.

The date of the start of Ramadan falls 10 to 12 days earlier each year. It is always the ninth month of the Islamic lunar calendar. A lunar month is shorter than a western month and starts when there is a full moon. In 2006 Ramadan started on 24 September, in 2007 it will be 12 September and in 2008, 2 September.

Ideally get a Muslim student or small group of students to explain what Ramadan is, why it exists and what it means to them. Alternatively, invite a speaker from the Islamic community, perhaps a parent, making it clear that you want only a five-minute (or shorter) presentation. Failing that, you can access the information at www.bbc.co.uk/schools/religion/islam/ramadan.shtml and tell the students more about Ramadan yourself.

You will need:
- Notes on Ramadan if you are providing all the information yourself
- Students carefully briefed, prepared and supported
- An outside speaker, met and looked after (possibly by students) during his or her visit.

This usually falls in early October. It celebrates animal life in all its forms and humankind's relationship with the animal kingdom. It is also about acknowledging the diverse roles that animals play in our lives, from providing food, through being our companions, to supporting and helping us and bringing a sense of wonder into our lives. There is lots of helpful information on the World Animal Day website www.worldanimalday.org.uk/

The best way to present this is to have a live animal to talk about as a starting point. If your school's health and safety rules will allow it, you (or a student) could bring in your own dog (or other pet) and introduce it. Failing that invite a blind person with a guide dog, a deaf person with a hearing dog or someone with another disability dog, or a police officer with a drug-sniffing dog. Health and safety rules always accommodate these and it's a good opportunity to illustrate the point that animals can be extremely useful in our everyday lives.

If none of that is possible, use pictures of domestic animals like dogs, sheep, donkeys, and wildlife such as tigers, stag beetles and toads which are part of the world's environment. Explain what they mean to you and why they matter. It's up to you and your outlook whether you mention food and humane farming. Another tack is to point out that there would be no food without insects, because they pollinate the crops, or talk just about dogs and all the different jobs they can do.

Finish with a reading of an animal poem such as 'Snake' by D. H. Lawrence, or 'Esther's Tomcat' by Ted Hughes.

Play out to a movement or two from *Carnival of the Animals* by Camille Saint-Saëns.

You will need:
- Live animal/or pictures and presentation
- An animal poem
- A recording of *Carnival of the Animals*.

ROSH HASHANAH

This is an assembly to mark the beginning of the Jewish New Year, which falls in September or October. Check the date from year to year. There are millions of Jewish people living all over the world, as well as in Israel. Rosh Hashanah, which lasts two days, celebrates the creation of the world. Jews say to each other 'L'shanah tovah' (for a good new year). Special services are held in synagogues, and in Jewish homes there's a special meal with the emphasis on sweetness – apples dipped in honey and a special sweet carrot stew with hallah bread are often served. Also on the table there is often a pomegranate. Pomegranates are supposed to have 613 seeds, so this is a symbol of the 613 commandments Jewish people have to follow.

Show a copy of the *Jewish Chronicle* newspaper. Say something about the diaspora and the state of Israel given to Jewish people in 1948. Explain what Jewish New Year involves and try to have as many Jewish items to show as possible, such as the Star of David, a skullcap and a Happy Jewish New Year greetings card. Talk a little about each.

In synagogues at Rosh Hashanah people hear the shofar, a ram's horn trumpet which plays a special rhythm on a hundred notes. There's a demo at www.bbc.co.uk/religion/religions/judaism/holydays/high_holy_days/rosh.shtml. Play this as part of the assembly.

Many Jewish people have suffered by being driven from their homes for many thousands of years. Have a minute's silence to think of people who have been exiled for whatever reason. End with a piece of Jewish Klezmer music or an extract from *Fiddler on the Roof* (the wedding party is the most exciting part).

You will need:
- ○ Notes on Rosh Hashanah
- ○ A copy of the *Jewish Chronicle*
- ○ The ram's horn demo
- ○ A recording of Jewish music.

On 5 November British people remember their lucky escape from what could have been a catastrophic event. In 1605, Catholic plotters, led by Robert Catesby, planned to blow up the Protestant Houses of Parliament at the State Opening (still held in November). They intended to kill King James I and everyone else gathered in the full house. Guido Fawkes, of Italian origin, was the explosives expert. Fortunately the plot was discovered and disaster averted, which is what we celebrate every year with fireworks and bonfires on 5 November.

Justice was harsh in those days. The plotters were tortured and then barbarically put to death. The details are all in Antonia Fraser's excellent book *The Gunpowder Plot*.

Give the assembly a modern angle by drawing parallels between England's near-miss in 1605 and more recent acts of terrorism. Perpetrators are usually passionate believers in their cause. Catesby and his followers were desperate to get the Catholics back into the centre of things. Muslim extremists, such as suicide bombers, give their lives in the cause of what they see as justice.

You could also read a short extract from *The Gunpowder Plot* and, from the same book, show pupils Guy Fawkes's two signatures, before and after he was tortured. It could be appropriate to have half a minute's silence to think about victims of torture.

Play out to part of *Music for the Royal Fireworks* by Handel.

You will need:
- Notes on the gunpowder plot and/or Antonia Fraser's book
- A recording of *Music for the Royal Fireworks*.

IDEA 23

WAR DEAD

This is for 11 November or a day close to it. About ten million young men died between 1914 and 1918 – British, German, French, Russian and many others. Many were the same age, or only a year or two older, than senior students in the school hall. After the war people wanted to remember the dead, so 11 November – the day peace was declared – became a special day. No one thinks war is a good thing, but once a war has happened we have to think about the needs of the people affected by it, such as widows, orphans and families.

Start your assembly by describing the horror of life at the front. Read aloud – or get a student to – 'Dulce et Decorum Est' by war poet Wilfred Owen. Go into as much or as little detail as is appropriate about what the 1914–18 war was and why it was fought. Show a red poppy used by the Royal British Legion for fundraising and explain that the Legion now raises money and helps to look after soldiers and families affected by all the wars since 1914–18.

Play part of the second movement of Beethoven's 3rd Symphony *Eroica*, which is based on a funeral march. Invite students to sit quietly and think about families anywhere in the world who are currently suffering terrible losses because of war.

You will need:
- ○ A copy of 'Dulce et Decorum Est'
- ○ A Royal British Legion poppy
- ○ A recording of Beethoven's *Eroica* symphony
- ○ Notes of the points you want to make about the 1914–18 war.

St Cecilia is the patron saint of music and her day is 22 November. Pieces of music and poems have been written in her honour and all over the world there are special concerts on this day.

According to the legend, Cecilia was a Christian in Rome in the early years of the Christian church. She refused to marry or to give up her faith and is said miraculously to have escaped several attempts to execute her. Eventually she was beheaded by a bungling executioner. She took three days to die, during which time she went on singing to God, hence the link with music.

Use the assembly to mark St Cecilia's day with music and explain why. Play three short extracts – if possible get the musical students to perform something. Try to get a variety such as:

ᴑ something by a current group or band likely be well known to the students
ᴑ something very light and silly such as 'Jingle Bells' or 'All I want for Christmas is me two front teeth'
ᴑ the opening of Mozart's Fortieth Symphony.

Make the point that music and musical taste includes everyone because it's so varied.

You will need:
ᴑ Notes on St Cecilia
ᴑ Recordings or performances of three contrasting pieces of music.

IDEA

25

DIWALI

Diwali is a five-day Hindu festival of light held during October or November. Its dates vary from year to year and it is also celebrated by Jains and Sikhs. It involves lights, fireworks, sweets and special meals. It's about the triumph of good over evil, light over darkness and knowledge over ignorance. Diwali is an important time of new beginnings. That's why participants spring-clean their homes, have new clothes and decorate the outsides of buildings with elaborate lights. Some of Britain's best Diwali celebrations are in the city of Leicester.

Because India is a large country, different legends have evolved in different parts of it. There are at least three accounts of the origins of Diwali. It could be a celebration of King Rama's arrival home after a 14-year war against the evil Ravana. Or it could have started with the rescue of the beautiful goddess Lakshmi from an evil king. Or perhaps Diwali celebrates the destruction of a terrible demon by the blue-skinned god Krishna.

Have the hall as dark as you can when the students arrive and have some Indian music playing. Then – perhaps using a group of rehearsed students to help you – suddenly create as many sorts of light as you can. Use Christmas tree lights, candles, torches, sparklers and, if there's space to do it safely, indoor fireworks. See if you can get the drama department to help you.

Explain to the audience that these lights are for Diwali and what they symbolize. Tell them that many Indian restaurants have special Diwali menus because there's an emphasis on delicious food during the celebrations. Eating one of these meals could be a way of taking part.

If you have Hindu students get two or three of them to tell the others what Diwali means to them and how they celebrate it. Otherwise there are video clips you can use at www.bbc.co.uk/leicester/videonation/archive/a_f/ dipak_joshi_my_diwali.shtml/

You will need:

- ○ A recording of Indian music
- ○ Various light sources
- ○ Notes on Diwali
- ○ Student presentations or video clips.

Thanksgiving is an annual celebration in the USA during the last weekend of November. Families assemble from all over the United States and abroad. They eat special meals and exchange presents.

North America was inhabited only by native people, mistakenly called Indians, when Europeans started to land and settle there from the early sixteenth century. The Europeans crossed the Atlantic Ocean in very uncomfortable, wooden sailing ships, some of which sank. They wanted to start a new life from scratch, but until they had built houses they had to live on the ships they had arrived in or in camps.

The early settlers went to what they called New England because it was the nearest to Europe. Wild turkeys were easily caught there. The settlers also found cranberries growing wild. Relieved to be safely on dry land, they caught and roasted a turkey and put some cooked cranberries with it. Then they thanked God in prayers for their safe arrival and held a little party to celebrate. It was the end of November and, in time, this became an annual event for Americans. Turkey and cranberry is still the traditional Thanksgiving dish.

Build an assembly around the origins and significance of Thanksgiving. If there is an American colleague or student to add personal anecdote to what you say, so much the better. Use an American flag as a prop and show the students a picture (perhaps via an electronic whiteboard) of the *Mayflower* or other early transatlantic vessel).

Play Louis Armstrong's 'What a Wonderful World' in which the most famous jazz singer of all time lists some of the things which make the world a good place.

You will need:
o Notes on Thanksgiving
o A recording of 'What a Wonderful World'
o An American flag
o A picture of the *Mayflower*.

This is for 1 December, or a date close to it. Everyone has heard of AIDS – **A**qcuired **I**mmune **D**eficiency **S**yndrome. It is a condition which stops a person's body naturally fighting infections, so he or she dies. It is caused by a virus – Human Immunodeficiency Virus or HIV – caught, usually by having unprotected sex, through the exchange of bodily fluids. People can have the virus for a long time before they get AIDS.

About 38.6 million people in the world are living with AIDS/HIV and around 2.8 million die from it each year. There are over 25 million sufferers in sub-Saharan Africa alone (2005 figures).

World AIDS Day is a time to think about these alarming figures. It's also a focus for thinking about how we can help. Particularly in need are AIDS orphans – children whose parents have died of AIDS – and there are many thousands of them in Africa. There is plenty of information on the World AIDS Day website (www. worldaidsday.com) about ways of getting involved, fundraising, human interest stories, wearing the red ribbon and so on.

For the assembly, share some of the shocking facts and statistics about AIDS and how it affects the families of the sufferers. It might make sense to use the assembly as a starting point for a (Christmas?) fundraising drive for an AIDS charity. A minute's silence to think about AIDS victims and their families would be appropriate.

You will need:
o Notes about AIDS and World AIDS Day.

IDEA

27

WORLD AIDS DAY

ADVENT

This is for early December, the season of Advent. It means 'coming'. Christians look forward to the coming of baby Jesus at Christmas. For most families shopping, cooking, present-wrapping and so on are part of a modern British Advent.

In the Church the season of Advent was traditionally regarded as the New Year. There are various sorts of new year which start on different dates: Chinese (usually in January/February), financial (6 April) school/academic (early September), Jewish (in September or October) and Church (early December – Advent), Islamic (date varies). 1 January is only one way of looking at it! The new year is usually a time for resolutions in all cultures.

Create an assembly by explaining the forward-looking significance of Advent. There are many customs to help us mark the passing of the time as we look forward. Show pupils as many sorts of Advent calendar as you can gather – religious ones with doors to open, secular ones with chocolates, or candles which have marks to burn down to each day.

Read aloud, or arrange for a student to recite, John Betjeman's poem 'Christmas' which begins 'The bells of waiting Advent ring'.

You will need:
○ Advent calendars
○ A copy of 'Christmas' by John Betjeman.

This is a very simple assembly idea which works well on any date during December. From *The Oxford Book of Christmas Stories*, edited by Dennis Pepper, read aloud 'The Christmas Gift' by Hugh Oliver. It takes only five or six minutes. It is about a modern Christmas Eve birth and speaks of death and life, hope and despair. It's best done with minimal preamble. Simply say that this is an appropriate story for the time of year which you find very powerful and which you want to share.

At the end just close the book and look at their faces. I find that a quiet remark such as, 'Well, I don't think that needs any further comment from me, do you?' is enough.

You could play them out to a thoughtful piece of Christmas music such a rendering of 'The Coventry Carol'.

You will need:
- A copy of *The Oxford Book of Christmas Stories*
- Music to end with if you wish.

IDEA

29

A CHRISTMAS STORY

FOR UNTO US A SON

This is another generic Christmas assembly for any date in December. Christmas – and the idea of a baby coming to do great things for the human race – has inspired many writers and musicians for many centuries.

When scholars in the fourth century made decisions about what to include in the Christian Bible they saw that much of the old Jewish teaching seemed to point ahead to the birth of Jesus. In Isaiah, 9.6–7, for example, the prophet looks forward to the coming of a messiah (saviour).

Of course, it wasn't originally written in English. Everything in the Bible took place in the Middle East, but various bits were translated over the years. In 1611, King James I ordered a group of scholars to translate the whole Bible into English for the first time. Many people read Isaiah, or heard it read aloud in church, so that it became very familiar to nearly everyone for hundreds of years.

In 1742, thousands of years after the writing of Isaiah, composer George Frederick Handel set those words to music. The music he wrote for 'For unto us a son in born' is one of the high spots of his famous oratorio, *Messiah*.

Create an assembly by linking the verses in Isaiah with Handel's lovely music. Read the passage from the Bible – or get a student to do so – and play the Handel piece for everyone to listen to.

You will need:
○ A Bible (the 1611 translation, also known as the Authorized or King James' Version.)
○ A recording of *Messiah*.

A focus on behaviour

COOPERATION

There is an old Chinese story about a man who dreamed he went to hell. There were big bowls of food, but everyone was starving because the chopsticks were six feet long so no one could pick up the food and bring it to his or her mouth. Then the man dreamed he went to heaven. There too everyone had a big bowl of food and a pair of six-foot long chopsticks. But no one was hungry and everyone was smiling and laughing, because they were using their chopsticks to feed each other.

Of course, you can add extra details to this outline story, such as what was in the bowls or what the people looked like. Draw the moral out of the story. People have to work together to survive and there are a lot of things you can't do on your own. Mention school examples, such as playing in a football team or singing in a choir, taking part in a play or keeping the atmosphere pleasant on the bus home.

Mention out-of-school examples of cooperation, such as family members helping each other, Neighbourhood Watch schemes, the United Nations. End with an encouraging statement such as, 'Try to find a new way of cooperating with those around you today.'

You will need:
o The Chinese story
o Notes on a card of the examples you want to mention.

THE GOOD SAMARITAN

The story of the Good Samaritan was told in the Bible by Jesus as a parable (St Luke 10.30–37). You can present it in its Christian context or simply as a stand-alone moral story about kindness and prejudice.

A man was travelling along the lonely road to Jericho when he was beaten up and robbed. Two respected members of the Jewish establishment passed by and ignored him. Then came a Samaritan, whose race was despised by the Jews. He helped the man to an inn, paid for his keep and told the innkeeper to keep a tally of any extra money spent so that he could settle the bill the next time he passed.

For your assembly, modernize the story and set it in your neighbourhood. Pick a road familiar to pupils. The passers-by could be, say, a teacher and a vicar, or a member of parliament and a nurse. The person who helps could be an illegal immigrant or a biker in scruffy leathers.

The morals to draw out of the story are that we should be kind to those in need (although youngsters have to be warned not to approach people in apparent need but to get help in case it's a trick) and that we must never judge people by appearances or by the group they belong to.

Both these can be related to the secondary school context. We should not judge other students (or teachers) without knowing them – give school-related examples if appropriate. Actions speak louder than words.

You will need:
o A prepared, modern version of the Good Samaritan story.

MAKING A DIFFERENCE

Florence Nightingale (1820–1910) took a team of nurses to Scutari (now Üsküdar, Turkey) in 1854 and reduced the Crimean War hospital's death rate from 42 per cent to 2 per cent. Later she founded the Nightingale School and Home for Nurses in London and is regarded as the founder of the modern nursing profession. She made a huge difference to many thousands of people.

In 1984, moved by images of young children in Africa dying of starvation, Bob Geldof organized a 'supergroup' of British musicians and singers which recorded the single 'Do They Know It's Christmas?' It became the fastest-selling single in UK history and raised over £8 million worldwide in funds for emergency aid to Ethiopia. In 2005 Bob Geldof organized the Live 8 concerts as part of his campaign for third world debt relief. He too is making a big difference to many people.

Base an assembly around the achievements of Nightingale, Geldof and, ideally, a local person known to the school. Stress the difference their actions have made.

Point out that everyone can make a difference to others and it doesn't have to be in a big or headline-grabbing way. If someone in school seems unhappy, try finding out what's wrong and seeing what you can do to help. Sometimes just a smile is all it takes to make a difference to someone. Or what about those who live near you? Or get involved in one of the charities supported by the school (give examples) or some of the charities which operate near your home. Try to find a way of making someone else's life better today.

Listen together to 'Do They Know It's Christmas?' and/or play it as the students leave.

You will need:
o Notes on Florence Nightingale and Bob Geldof
o Examples of how students could make a difference
o A recording of 'Do They Know It's Christmas?'

This needs careful, advance planning. Quietly find six willing students who will be in your assembly and who have a physical characteristic such as being over six feet tall or having red hair. Give each of them something very distinctive to wear in the assembly, like a large red ribbon on a safety pin. Explain that you are going to 'abuse' them in assembly, but that it's all a piece of drama – and swear them to secrecy.

When you take the assembly be very stern and deadpan. Say something like, 'There are six people in this room who are . . . blonde, left-handed or whatever . . . and they're wearing badges so that we all know who they are.' Order them to stand up and then 'abuse' them. Tell them that neither you nor any student in the school likes them, so they will, in future, have to have separate lessons, eat their food in a special place, etc. If they get bullied you, for one, don't care. Ham it up as much as you like for as long as seems appropriate.

Then come out of role, thank your six 'victims' (give them a round of applause?) and explain that you are making a point about racism – it's arbitrary, personal, pointless and cruel. Anyone who fails to respect another person because he or she is of a different race is behaving as unreasonably as you were just now.

Martin Luther King campaigned for equality for blacks in the southern states of the USA until he was assassinated in 1968. Play a recording of his famous 'I have a dream' speech. It's available on CD and cassette, along with other famous speeches.

Negro spirituals were the songs made up and sung by black slaves to keep their spirits up. Play a recording of one, such as 'Swing Low, Sweet Chariot' or 'Go Down, Moses'.

You will need:
- ○ Six carefully briefed students
- ○ A recording of 'I have a dream'
- ○ A recording of a negro spiritual.

COURTESY

Rehearse three pairs of students in advance. Pair one has a 30-second sketch or mime in which one student holds open a door for the other who is carrying something heavy or awkward. Pair two is buying something at a shop and deciding which student is first in the queue. Pair three has to act out a scene where one person has sent a birthday gift the previous week and the recipient of the present is now saying thank you. Each sketch could be done several times with different roles. Pair one might start, for example, by being a student opening a door for a teacher carrying a pile of books, or two shoppers in a department store. The students themselves will be able to think of plenty of situations.

Then point out to the assembly that courtesy – politeness and thoughtfulness to others – applies wherever and whoever you are. Students should be courteous to each other as well as to adults. It makes life better for everyone. And if someone fails to show courtesy to you it doesn't mean that you have a right not to be courteous or that you lower your own standards. Rise above it and behave better than he or she did. Saying 'Thank you' and smiling make a big difference to the way humans react to one another. Try it.

Listen to a recording of 'Thank U Very Much' by The Scaffold. Then use it as play-out music.

You will need:
o Students with prepared sketches
o A recording of 'Thank U Very Much'.

In a family consisting of grandfather, father, mother and one child, the grandfather is getting old, frail and messy. The mother gets irritated with her father-in-law and makes him eat his food on the floor from a dog's wooden bowl. One day she finds her young son making something from wood. When asked what he is doing he says, 'I'm making a wooden bowl ready for you and father when you get old.' This makes her see how cruel she has been and she invites the father-in-law back to the family table where she looks after him properly.

Tell this story, perhaps modernized, with as much colour and detail as you like. Then draw out the morals: 1) we should be kind to older people; 2) we should respect them; 3) good behaviour is role-modelled and passed on from one generation to another; 4) we get out of life what we put in or, as the Bible puts it, we 'reap what we sow'. You might also mention the fifth commandment given to the Jews by Moses, 'Honour your father and mother'. (Exodus. 20. 12)

Read aloud (or get a student to) the poem 'My Grandmother' by Elizabeth Jennings.

Play out to part of 'Saturn, the Bringer of Old Age' from *The Planets* by Gustav Holst.

You will need:
o Your version of the folk story about the family and the wooden bowls
o 'My Grandmother' by Elizabeth Jennings
o A recording of *The Planets*.

RESPECT FOR THE ELDERLY

BRAVERY

Group Captain Douglas Bader DSO DFC (1910–82) lost both legs in a daredevil flying accident in the 1930s. But he still joined the RAF and distinguished himself in World War Two, because he was both determined and brave, which are good qualities to emulate. He was captured by the Germans in 1941. He tried to escape so often that in the end they put him in the supposedly impregnable Colditz Castle. He was liberated from there by the allies in 1945. After the war he was a tireless worker for amputees and was knighted for this work in 1976.

His life before and during the war is told in the book *Reach for the Sky* by Paul Brickhill. It was made into a classic film starring Kenneth More in 1956. (You can buy a DVD of this or, almost certainly borrow it from your public library.)

Make an assembly out of Bader's story, stressing his bravery in refusing to let his personal difficulties stand in the way of what he wanted to do. Read aloud an extract from Paul Brickhill's book or, if facilities are available, show a clip from the film.

End with a minute's silence to think about the problems of amputees, especially those injured by landmines, in troubled parts of the world.

You will need:
o Notes on Douglas Bader
o *Reach for the Sky* book and/or DVD.

Walk into assembly with a pocket or bag full of scrap paper, sweet wrappers, perhaps a banana skin, pizza box and so on. Drop or throw it about very obviously so that the students notice. They will probably laugh because this is very odd behaviour for a teacher.

Ask students what they have noticed about streets in most countries apart from Britain. Draw out of them that many places, especially in Europe and the USA, seem to have much less street litter than the UK. Many tonnes of rubbish, such as takeaway food wrapping, cigarette packets and newspapers, are dropped in Britain every day, on country roads from cars, as well as in towns. Give local examples of where the problem is particularly acute. Schools are the same. Mention a part of the school where litter is habitually dropped.

Talk about the filthy pollution of litter and, as an alternative, about paper recycling. Mention the specifics of how paper can be recycled in the school area. Mention bins in and out of school and explain that good litter-bin behaviour has to be demonstrated to younger children so that they don't grow up thinking that dropping litter is acceptable.

You may remember the Wombles when you were younger. What great role models! They lived under Wimbledon Common and their 'work' was collecting and recycling rubbish. Read aloud a passage from one of Elizabeth Beresford's Womble books in which the creatures are gathering litter. You could play out to 'The Wombling Song', first heard as the signature tune to the TV series in 1974.

Don't forget to gather up the litter you dropped at the beginning of the assembly and put it in the bin.

You will need:
o Some litter and a bin
o An extract from a Wombles book
o A recording of 'The Wombling Song'.

In 1941 a Jewish teenager was spotted on the stairs with his father in a house in Berlin being raided by Nazi soldiers. Most of the Jews were taken to camps and the majority sent to their deaths in gas chambers. In this case there was a pause. Then the soldier looked at the boy, smiled and deliberately looked the other way, so the boy and his father escaped. Eventually they arrived in England and the boy grew up to be quite a well-known journalist. He owed his life to a moment of kindness from an unexpected quarter.

Have you been kind to anyone today? Have you smiled at someone who looks unhappy, helped someone to carry something heavy or listened to someone's problems? If everyday life is a patchwork quilt, kindness is the stitching which holds it together (show a patchwork item if you have one). Without kindness life falls apart. Tell the students an anecdote about when someone was kind to you and what a difference it made.

Being kind means treating others as you would like to be treated yourself. So if you see someone sitting alone in the dining room, take your tray over, say 'Hi!' and join him or her. Imagine how you might feel if you thought no one wanted to sit with you. Jesus, in the Bible, tells his followers that they should treat others as they would like to be treated.

Read aloud the story of Jesus healing the girl who is apparently dead at Capernaum. Not only does Jesus bring her out of her coma or deep sleep, but he is very kind to the family. He is also kind to the sick woman who delays him on his way to Capernaum (St Mark 5.21–43)

End with half a minute's silence to think about kindness. Then play out to something gentle and thoughtful, such as Mozart's *Clarinet Concerto*.

You will need:
o Notes of points you plan to make
o The extract from St Mark
o A patchwork item (not essential)
o Suitable music to end with.

Have a class of students sitting on chairs in pairs, facing forward to form a bus. At the front someone is driving. In turn the passengers throw down litter, stand up, jostle and shout at each other, throw things, bully a young student sitting alone, are rude to an elderly passenger, stand on the seats, scratch the windows, scribble on the notices and shout out of open windows. When they get off they shout abuse at the driver.

Then run the 'bus' again. This time the students display the opposite behaviour. They sit quietly talking to the person next to them, they exchange a smile and a pleasant word with the solitary student and elderly passenger. They don't drop litter or vandalize the bus, and when they get off they thank the driver.

Thank your 'actors'. Point out to the assembly that it is completely obvious which sort of behaviour is the right one. Buses are places where people are confined in a small space and for a few minutes they can't get away. Mutual respect is essential for everyone's comfort and safety. Link your comments to citizenship education if appropriate. Point out that the same principles apply to trains, trams, tubes and all other public transport.

End by listening to Flanders and Swann's song 'Transport of Delight' ('A big six-wheeler, scarlet-painted, London Transport, diesel-engined, 97 horsepower omnibus') from *At the Drop of a Hat*.

You will need:
o About 20 students rehearsed to demonstrate good and bad bus behaviour
o CD of *At the Drop of a Hat*.

BEHAVIOUR ON PUBLIC TRANSPORT

BULLYING

Read aloud the poem 'The Place's Fault' by Philip Hobsbaum (1932–2005). The boy in the poem is remembering a time when he was desperately unhappy because he was bullied by a group of boys from another school.

Why do some people want to make others unhappy? Often it is because they are jealous or unhappy themselves in some way. Remember that bullying often starts as teasing – a harmless joke – and then grows into something which really upsets the 'victim'. Often it involves a group turning against one person.

Sadly, it happens wherever there are human beings – in workplaces and even school staffrooms (but fortunately not in this school!), as well as in schools. At this point, I usually tell an anecdote about being bullied by a much older teacher when I was a young teacher in a different school far from here, stressing how it felt and how unhappy it made me.

We have to work together to prevent bullying, and basically that means being aware of each other's needs and being kind. It means also telling someone if you feel you are being victimized or you know someone else who is. It is a hard thing to stop, but we can do it if we work together.

End with a reading of 'The Lesson' by Edward Lucie Smith (born 1933). It is another poem about a deeply unhappy, bullied child.

You will need:
o Copies of 'The Place's Fault' and 'The Lesson'
o A note of the points you want to make.

Born in 1902, Gladys Aylward was a Christian. She believed she had to go to China to help people there, but she was only a servant in London and was rejected by the missionary organization she applied to. Eventually she went independently to China via the trans-Siberian railway in the early 1930s. After the invasion by the Japanese she led a group of orphaned Chinese children on a dangerous journey to safety – an outstanding example of what you can achieve if you really believe that you have to do something.

Show a clip of the classic 1958 film *The Inn of the Sixth Happiness*, starring Ingrid Bergman, which is about Gladys Aylward's life. (You can buy a DVD of this or almost certainly borrow it from your public library.) Show the bit when she is leading the children in faith.

Few students in the assembly will feel the need to travel quite as far as Gladys Aylward, but everyone can stand up for what they believe in. If you are committed to something, then be proud of it. If you want better conditions for political prisoners worldwide, join Amnesty International and find out what you can do to help. If you're uncomfortable about the killing of animals for food, become a vegetarian. Convictions, if carefully thought out, are good things to have. Practise them with courage!

End with a minute's silence to remember the life and work of Gladys Aylward and others like her and the people they help.

You will need:
○ DVD of *The Inn of the Sixth Happiness,* in the right place
○ Notes on Gladys Aylward.

STANDING UP FOR YOUR BELIEFS

PATIENCE, WISDOM AND VISION

Born 18 July 1918, Nelson Mandela was imprisoned for 27 years for crimes against the state of South Africa. He was freed in 1990 as political opinion began to change. In 1994 Mandela became South Africa's first black president in the country's first democratic elections. He stepped down in 1999, but continued to work to reduce AIDS/HIV in Africa and to help diplomatic work in other African countries.

Mandela is famous and widely revered for his patience, wisdom and vision, qualities he seemed to acquire and develop during those long years in prison.

We can emulate these qualities. We can be patient with people who irritate us and not always expect everything to be as we want it immediately (use an example from the school context). We can try to become wise and to admire wisdom in those who already have it. It often involves listening, thinking and trying to see things from different viewpoints, rather than giving in to knee-jerk responses (give a school-based example).

And let's be visionary. We need to know how, eventually, we would like things to be, however long it takes. Relate this to a school context and give an example.

Finish with this old, multi-faith 'prayer' to God – whatever, or however, you conceive him to be:

'May I have the courage to change the things I can, the patience to bear with the things I can't – and the wisdom to know the difference.'

You will need:
o Notes on Nelson Mandela
o Notes of points you wish to make
o The prayer written down.

Play a recording of a choir singing the hymn 'Dear Lord and Father of Mankind'. The 'still small voice of calm' in the last verse is what the Old Testament prophet Elijah eventually found – and we could all do with.

Then read the words of Psalm 23, also about calm, peace and tranquillity.

Then read aloud this modern version:

The Lord is my pacesetter, I shall not rush
He makes me to stop and rest for quiet intervals.
He provides me with images of stillness which restore
*   my serenity.*
He leads me in ways of efficiency, through calmness of
*   mind. And his guidance is peace.*
Even though I have a great many things to accomplish
*   each day I will not fret.*
For his presence is here; his timeliness, his all
*   importance will keep me in balance.*
He prepares refreshment and renewal for me in the
*   midst of activity*
By anointing my mind with his oil of tranquillity. My
*   cup of joyous energy overflows.*
Surely harmony and effectiveness shall be the fruit of
*   my hours.*
For I shall walk in the pace of my Lord forever.

The writer wants to work hard and achieve things, but is also asking his/her god to make sure that he/she remains calm and doesn't let things get out of proportion. We could try to hang on to a sense of calm and proportion as we rush about finishing coursework, getting to a football practice or staff meeting, or writing next year's timetable (use your own topical examples).

If you have the facilities and commitment to sing a hymn, end with singing 'Dear Lord and Father of Mankind' together. If not, play again the recording of it.

You will need:
o The original and the modern versions of Psalm 23
o A recording of, and/or facilities to sing 'Dear Lord and Father of Mankind'.

STILL SMALL VOICE OF CALM

IDEA 45

You can often make an assembly from a current newspaper story. This is an example from an August 2006 newspaper. Try using a similar framework to create an assembly based on something currently in the news. It is worth keeping cuttings and putting possible behaviour-related assembly stories from newspapers into a ringbinder. Many will stay current for a few weeks.

An English woman in her twenties rode with her boyfriend and a team of six horses 2,000 miles across the Australian desert, from the west to the east coast. It took four months and she was the first English woman – and probably the first woman ever – to have achieved this. It is an upbeat story with messages about courage, determination, endurance, imagination, physical strength and so on. You can share your thoughts on such projects and link the attributes she showed to the school context. Then finish with a suitable piece of music, in this case something relating to horses, riding or Australia.

You will need:
o The story you've chosen to retell
o Pictures to illustrate the story if you can blow them up large enough, perhaps via an electronic whiteboard
o Music which fits the theme.

The young men of a tribe – in some remote part of the world – couldn't stop quarrelling. Their chief was very worried about what would happen after his death, so he got each young man to bring a stick to the next meeting. He bound all the sticks together with string and then asked each young man in turn to try to break the bundle across his knee. None could. Then the chief untied the bundle and passed each man a single stick with the same invitation. Of course the separate sticks broke easily. The leader then told the young men that a person who quarrels and stands alone is easily broken, but that those who stand together will have great strength.

Retell the folk story above, adding as much corroborative detail as you wish. Modernize it (to include women, for instance) if you prefer. You could even present a practical, or dramatized, demonstration with a bundle of sticks. The message, of course, is, 'United we stand, divided we fall' and/or 'Many things/creations/organizations are much greater than the sum of their parts'.

Link this to working together as a form group, a problem-solving group in a lesson, the school council, the school itself, the family, or any other group with a common purpose. Play a thoughtful piece of music, such as the first movement of Beethoven's *Moonlight Sonata*, as background and invite the students to think, as they listen, about the advantages of harmonious cooperation.

You will need:
○ Your version of the sticks-in-bundles story
○ Notes of the points you wish to make about working together
○ Contemplative music.

COMPASSION

Elizabeth Fry (1780–1845) worked all her life to improve conditions for prisoners, especially women at Newgate prison in London. In Fry's day prisoners were kept in the most appalling conditions. She was the wife of Joseph Fry. They were Quakers and connected with the Fry's chocolate-making business. Quakers are Christians who believe in quiet meditation and very simple services without set prayers. They have long been associated with compassion, caring and giving. Elizabeth Fry helped women inmates to look after children imprisoned with their mothers and provided them with clothing, food and basic education. Later she also worked to improve conditions for convicts being transported to Australia and for homeless people in London and Brighton.

Tell the assembly about Elizabeth Fry's life, adding as much detail as appropriate, and her work – still unfinished. Prisoners are still kept in overcrowded conditions which many people regard as unacceptable. The Howard League for Penal Reform still struggles to get things improved. Give examples of twenty-first century conditions – 20 hours a day locked in a cell with a toilet in the same room; two or three people kept in cells meant for one; not allowed to vote, etc. Alternatively, for this, or perhaps for a subsequent assembly, you might invite a speaker from the Howard League.

The main point is: yes, people in prison are guilty of crimes, sometimes very serious crimes, which they need not have committed, but they still have rights as human beings. This is related to behaviour because its aim is to foster compassion in the students. End with a minute's silence to think about prisoners and their families.

You will need:
○ Notes on Elizabeth Fry
○ Notes on the Howard League and modern prison conditions.

REPAIRING DAMAGE

This is an assembly about repairing damage and is another example of how you can create assembly material from the news. In January 2006 Nick Flynn, a member of the public, tripped on some steps at the Fitzwilliam Museum in Cambridge. He fell against, and smashed, a rare and valuable seventeenth-century Chinese porcelain vase from the Qing Dynasty. In August 2006 it was reported that specialist ceramic restorer Penny Bendall had glued together 113 pieces. She taped all the pieces together and bound them with a special adhesive before applying a final polish and coating of enamel. The vase then went back on display.

At the time this seemed to be an irrevocable disaster which, like many problems in life, couldn't be mended, but it has been. That vase could stand as a metaphor for 'broken'.

For example, a quarrel between friends could seem to be a permanent break, but perhaps the pieces can be glued back? If a friend gets into serious trouble, perhaps with the police, how can you help him or her to glue his/her life back together? Give other examples, perhaps specific to the school.

Show the sequence in the film *Nanny McPhee* when the children wreck the kitchen and everything seems to be beyond repair. And remind them that the film has a happy ending.

Play 'Could We Start Again Please?' from *Jesus Christ Superstar* for everyone to listen to and perhaps repeat it as the students file out.

You will need:
○ Notes on the Fitzwilliam Museum vase
○ A DVD of *Nanny McPhee*, in the right place
○ A recording of *Jesus Christ Superstar*, in the right place.

IDEA 49

Get a group of students to rehearse and present an improvised mini-play in which they are misbehaving in a classroom or other school space. Unacceptable language is flying about but f—, c——, s—— and p—— words are replaced by silly, invented words such as frell, cond, stap and pafe. So the play's dialogue is full of 'frell off', 'frilling cond', 'don't give me that stap!', 'Pafe off'. The students will have fun preparing this and it should be hilarious when presented to the school.

When the laughter subsides the points to make are:

o It is possible to sound very rude or abusive, even when the words are meaningless. It's often the tone of voice which is offensive.
o Some words are socially unacceptable and every one of us knows it, which is why we laughed just now.
o It isn't very logical to be offended by some words and not at all offended by others.
o It gets boring to listen to the same words over and over again – it shows a very limited vocabulary. Sadly, that is often the case with people who rely on taboo words. They want to shock, but, also, they don't know many other words!
o Try to get into the habit of choosing accurate words which say what you really mean, rather than lazily relying on a handful.
o Courteous people always consider the feelings of the people they are talking to and of others nearby.

Play out to 'The Major-General's Song' from *The Pirates of Penzance* by W. S. Gilbert and Arthur Sullivan – an example of extensive vocabulary in action.

You will need:
o The rehearsed play
o A recording of 'The Major-General's Song'.

Read aloud the biblical story of Solomon and the two women arguing over a baby's maternity. (1Kings 3.16–28) Solomon offers to cut the baby in two so that each woman can have half. Explain, if necessary, the point of Solomon's judgement. He knows that the real mother, whichever she is, will never consent to the division of the child. Solomon, in the Bible, was the son of King David and Bathsheba and a great king much admired for his wisdom. He also built a great temple.

We must all try to be good and tough judges of character and situations in our everyday lives. It comes partly with experience. But you don't have to be old to be wise! Give simple, school-based examples.

According to the biblical story, Solomon was, at one point, visited by the exotic Queen of Sheba. Composer George Frederick Handel (1685–1759) featured this in his oratorio, *Solomon*. Play the 'Arrival of the Queen of Sheba' for students to listen to.

You will need:
- A Bible (any version)
- Notes about wisdom
- A recording of the 'Arrival of the Queen of Sheba'.

WISDOM AND JUDGEMENT

SECTION
3

Topical issues

IDEA 51

FAMINE

Ask exactly 69 students (probably two classes plus a few more) to stand in a block at the front, along the side on the stage, wherever it's convenient and where the rest of the assembly can see them clearly. Count them off into three groups of 23. Time one minute, then ask 23 to sit down. Repeat this twice more until three minutes have passed and the whole group has 'gone'. You could play a piece of very solemn music such as the 'Dead March' from Handel's *Saul* while this is going on. This exercise illustrates that 23 children, somewhere in the world, die of hunger every minute – six million every year.

Also, 840 million people do not have enough to eat, and of these, 153 million are under five. 51 nations do not produce enough food for their own people. About 10 per cent of the cause is drought, floods, wars or political/social/economic factors. Otherwise the problem is poverty. You can flesh out these facts if you wish at www.care.org/campaigns/world-hunger/facts.asp/

Mention dieting and the obsession with body shape in rich countries. What an irony that one half of the world starves while the other becomes obese. Show some famine pictures, perhaps via an electronic whiteboard.

If appropriate, use this assembly to launch school fundraising for one of the developing world charities. The chosen charity would probably be happy to supply a speaker for another assembly later on.

End with a minute's silence to think of the X number of children who have died in the X minutes that this assembly has lasted. Work out the number. A nine-minute assembly means 207 dead; 10 minutes is 230, 11 is 253, 12 is 276, 13 is 299, 14 is 322, 15 is 345.

You will need:
○ Solemn music
○ Facts about famine
○ Famine pictures.

CLIMATE CHANGE

Scientists tell us that the world is getting hotter. Ice is melting in the Arctic Circle in summer much more than it used to and then it's failing to freeze up fully in winter – difficult for animals like polar bears. Bananas have been known to ripen in Britain outdoors in recent years, and we see exotic butterflies which used not to come to Britain. All over the world there is freak weather – fill in with recent examples.

Some scientists say that all this is part of the world's normal pattern of change. It has always got hotter and colder at different times. Others say that the changes we have now are happening much faster than in the ancient past. They think it is caused by human beings gobbling up resources and burning fossil fuels which produce destructive emissions.

So what should we do, apart from using sun block, buying thinner clothes and being thankful we don't need to wear coats as often as our grandparents did? Each of us can help in tiny ways which add up to something bigger if enough people take part. We can try not to use too much fuel – walk more and use vehicles less – and recycle paper products to save trees.

Have six students ready to make everyday resource-saving suggestions such as, 'Offer to walk to the primary school to collect your kid brother to save your mum using the car', or 'Always buy recycled paper when you get a pad or notebook.' The main message is that everyone can make a difference, however small.

Meanwhile, let's enjoy the wildlife that a warmer climate brings. End with a reading – either by you or by a student – of 'The Zebras' by Roy Campbell.

You will need:
- ○ Notes on climate change
- ○ Students ready to present six 'green' ideas
- ○ 'The Zebras' for reading aloud.

CRUELTY TO ANIMALS

At different times in the past badger-baiting, cock-fighting, bear-baiting, dog fights, rat-killing by dogs for sport, dancing bears, hare-coursing and hunting otters were all legal. You may need to explain what some of these involved. Today they are all against the law.

The Royal Society for the Prevention of Cruelty to Animals (RSPCA) started in the nineteenth century. It keeps an eye on places where animals are held, used or kept, such as farms, catteries, dog and horse racing tracks, slaughter houses, people's homes – make your own list, ideally drawing it from the students. It also takes in unwanted, ill-treated and abandoned animals and tries to find suitable new homes for them. The RSPCA also campaigns against practices it would like to see made totally illegal, such as stag and fox hunting, which are still allowed under some circumstances.

Attitudes are different in many other countries. For instance, bull fighting is legal in Spain and France, animals still perform in circuses in Europe, and China has no laws covering animal welfare so no one is ever prosecuted for being cruel to an animal. In all these countries there are people who want changes.

It is silly to pretend that animals are just humans with fur (or feathers or scales) but they deserve respect. Nineteenth-century thinker Jeremy Bentham said, 'The question is not how much an animal can feel, but can it suffer?'

There is enough material in all this for several assemblies. Just decide how much detail you want to present. There is also scope for inviting a speaker from the RSPCA or one of the other animal charities. Alternatively you might get a small group of students to mount a presentation for an assembly on, for example, the pros and cons of battery hens or zoos.

Finish with an extract from John Masefield's poem 'Reynard the Fox' read by you or a student.

You will need:
○ Notes on cruelty to animals
○ Students with presentations or an outside speaker
○ A copy of 'Reynard the Fox'.

Play the 1960's Lonnie Donegan number 'My Old Man's a Dustman'. Then introduce the question of where the rubbish goes once the 'refuse collector' has taken it away. Most goes to landfill sites – huge holes in which the rubbish is buried. There are nearly 20,000 such sites in Britain, and 80 per cent of the population lives within 2 km of one.

We can't go on burying rubbish for ever. It is not sustainable. Some of it doesn't rot and there is some evidence that living near a landfill site can cause, or make worse, some illnesses. So, we have to limit what we send to landfill.

Get the students to consider the alternatives. Have a group of students ready to mention in turn things like: composting vegetable waste, recycling paper, plastic bottles, tins, cartons and so on, trying to buy things with less packaging, re-using carrier bags, avoiding disposable items (nappies could be a controversial one). Most households, and schools, could probably cut by three-quarters what they send via the dustman to landfill sites.

Finish by playing the Lonnie Donegan song again.

You will need:
o A recording of 'My Old Man's a Dustman'
o Students with suggestions for minimizing dustbin use.

NOT IN THE DUSTBIN

In *David Copperfield* by Charles Dickens, Mr Micawber is charming. He has a devoted wife and many children, but he is hopeless with money and always in debt. He even spends time (as Dickens's father did in real life) in a debtors' prison. Eventually he gives David some advice. Read it aloud to the assembly. It begins, 'My other piece of advice, Copperfield . . .' and it's about halfway through Chapter 12.

When debt gets out of control it is deeply distressing, as some students in the hall will know. Mention house repossession and insolvency in general terms if it's right for your students or tell an anecdote about yourself or a 'friend' so you distance it from the students.

If appropriate, you might talk a little about debt avoidance and trying not to hanker for things which you can't pay for, but it has to be balanced against the adult necessity of mortgages and, these days, student loans. You could illustrate the points with student role-plays showing different kinds of debt, such as unpaid bills, bank overdraft, and a loan from a friend.

Then tell them about debt counsellors, not to be confused with 'advisers' who actually may be 'loan sharks' charging very high interest rates. You can find a debt counsellor via the Citizens Advice Bureau. It is worth drawing students' attention to the CAB and some of the services it can offer.

Play Abba's 'Money, Money, Money' to finish.

You will need:
○ A copy of *David Copperfield*
○ Notes on debt
○ A recording of 'Money, Money, Money'.

Ask everyone in the room to close his/her eyes tightly for about 30 seconds. They should feel the texture of their clothing and listen to sounds in the hall and in the distance. Can anyone smell floor polish or food? This, in a tiny way, is how it might feel to be blind.

Consider some famous blind people. Helen Keller (1890–1968) of the USA had no sight or hearing and never really learned to speak. Her loss was the result of an illness, probably meningitis, at 19 months old. Exceptionally bright, and with the support of her inspirational teacher Anne Sullivan, she became a world-famous writer, lecturer and fundraiser.

Louis Braille (1809–1852) lost the sight of one eye in an accident and the second eye in an infection – all before his fourth birthday. He invented an embossed system of reading and writing based on six raised dots felt with the fingertips. It is still in use worldwide.

David Blunkett MP was Secretary of State for Education and Skills from 1997–2001 and then Home Secretary. He uses a guide dog and all his documents are translated into Braille.

Build an assembly around inspiring stories about people who overcome blindness. You may be able to flesh it out with people known to the students. Even better, invite a blind person, perhaps with a guide dog, to the assembly.

Blindness anecdotes are useful. For example, I used to go square dancing with two blind teenagers, and their ability to know where everyone was in the dance was astonishing.

If appropriate, this assembly could launch a fundraising project, perhaps for one of the charities which funds cataract operations in the developing world where blindness is a widespread problem.

End with a minute's silence to think about the needs, problems and achievements of blind people everywhere.

You will need:
o Notes on famous blind people.

IDEA 57

THE BIG ISSUE

Get two students to act out a street scene prepared in advance. One sells copies of *The Big Issue*, the other is a kindly customer. The customer will buy the magazine for the exact price, check the vendor's badge and ask him or her a few friendly questions.

Have two or three copies of *The Big Issue* magazine to hold up. Started by former homeless man John Bird, The Big Issue is a company which offers work to homeless people, or those in 'vulnerable' housing, so that they don't have to beg. They pay about 60p for each magazine (payable afterwards) and sell it for £1.40, so we should all buy it as often as we can because it's a good way to help. Make sure that the vendor is registered with a badge, and be friendly.

Mr Bird called his magazine *The Big Issue* because homelessness is a major problem in Britain and many other countries. He tried to do something practical about it. Read aloud from the magazine one of the pieces written by a vendor. You could also talk about the work of the Salvation Army, which tries to help homeless people get off the streets. End with a moment's silence to think about the plight of homeless people.

You will need:
- ○ Students with a Big Issue sketch
- ○ Copies of *The Big Issue*
- ○ Notes on John Bird and the company he started
- ○ Notes on the Salvation Army's work with the homeless.

Read aloud Thomas Hardy's poem 'Throwing a Tree'.

It takes hundreds of years for some trees to reach their full height. Mention some mature trees near the school and make a comparison with when they would have been planted, for example, when George III was king and Jane Austen was writing her books in the early 1800s.

It takes a tree-feller only an hour or so to chop down a large tree. Of course, it's sometimes acceptable to cut down trees for their wood, but it has to be done in a way that is sustainable so that new trees grow at the same rate as old ones are cut down. In this way there will always be trees, woods and forests. In practice that means planting fast-growing trees and leaving slow-growing ones, such as oak, alone. That's why we see fast-growing saplings beside motorways and in open spaces; they are an attempt to create new forests. When you buy anything made of wood it's good to look for a label which guarantees that only sustainable forest was used.

Get a student to research and present some statistics about the rapid destruction of forests in South America, especially in the Amazon. There is plenty of information on the Internet.

Listen to and/or play out to 'Bohemia's Woods and Forests' from *Má Vlast* by Bedrich Smetana.

You will need:
- A copy of 'Throwing a Tree'
- Notes on forests
- Student with Amazon statistics
- A recording of *Má Vlast*.

INDIA'S RAILWAY CHILDREN

Use an electronic whiteboard to show pictures of railway children in India (see www.railwaychildren.org.uk).

Read this aloud or retell it in your own words. Four-year-old Kalyan was found abandoned on a railway station platform in India. He was taken to a shelter in Hyderabad where he was diagnosed as HIV positive. He was given medical attention and looked after by a project run by the charity Railway Children. Kalyan later died, not alone on the streets, but surrounded by people who loved and cared for him.

Railway Children's UK Chief Executive, Terina Keene, says, 'In India the train is the biggest mode of transport – the railways carry 11 million people a day. Everybody moves around the country by train. It's no surprise that children also move around by train. Many children who land in big cities and towns, having run away, been lost, abandoned or missing, are found around transport terminals every day' (from www.community care.co.uk where there is more information).

Draw attention to the predicament of children who live rough on Indian railway stations. You could include: acted-out stories based on case studies taken from websites, examples from websites read aloud, Indian music (perhaps something by Ravi Shankar) and a minute's silence.

You will need:
o Pictures of railway children and the means to display them
o Stories about railway children in whichever way you decide to present them
o Indian music.

Play a recording of the hymn 'Eternal Father, Strong to Save'.

Talk about the dangers faced by seamen. Tell the story of Grace Darling (1815–42), the lighthouse keeper's daughter who helped her father to rescue nine people in a terrible storm off Bamburgh, Northumberland in 1838. You could mention the sinking of the channel ferry, *The Herald of Free Enterprise*, off the Belgian coast near Zeebrugge in 1987, when 193 people died.

Talk about the work of the Royal National Lifeboats Institution (RNLI) (see www.rnli.org.uk), which has 233 stations in the UK and Ireland manned by volunteers. You could also invite an RNLI speaker.

Finish by playing the hymn again or, if it's appropriate, it would be better still to sing it. Even if you are listening to a recording you could display the words on an electronic whiteboard.

You will need:
o Notes on Grace Darling
o Information about, or a speaker from, the RNLI
o Recording and words of 'Eternal Father, Strong to Save'.

FOR THOSE IN PERIL ON THE SEA

TRANSPORT RESOURCES

Have a group of students rehearsed and ready to list, taking turns, all the ways in which we can use less fuel for transport: walk more, cycle more, use smaller cars, use electric cars, use cars which run on methane, don't go out so much, make fewer journeys by air, and so on.

Have another group of students ready with a short presentation giving the statistics about fossil fuels and sustainability.

Have a third group of students prepared to explain briefly what effect overuse of fossil fuel transport has on the environment: noise pollution by aircraft, as well as airports, roads and railway lines on rural land.

Every little counts. Each one of us could walk short journeys. How far do you live from school? We could try to shop locally rather than driving to supermarkets (whose wares are transported in large, polluting lorries). Any student working with you will be able to think of more possibilities.

You will need:
o Students with a list of environmentally friendly alternatives
o Students with facts about fossil fuels
o Students with facts about transport damaging the environment.

Start with a vote. How many students would like to see the death penalty – hanging or a lethal injection – brought back for serious crimes such as murder?

There will be a division of opinion, possibly around 50/50. Explain that until the 1860s there were public hangings in Britain. The last hanging (behind closed doors) was in 1964 and the last woman hanged was Ruth Ellis in 1955. Add as much background information as is appropriate.

Then talk about some famous miscarriages of justice such as John Christie and Timothy Evans (www.bbc.co.uk/crime/caseclosed/rillingtonplace.shtml) and Christopher Craig and Derek Bentley (www.stephen-stratford.co.uk/derek_bentley.htm). Mention recent cases and decisions such as Saddam Hussein.

Have two students prepared to list reasons for and against the death penalty (such as the cost of keeping someone in prison indefinitely, and that there is no way of correcting mistakes). Make it clear that there are no easy answers, but many different opinions.

Ask the students to vote again at the end. Is there anyone who has changed their mind, in either direction, because of anything said in the assembly?

You will need:
○ Background information about capital punishment
○ Notes on famous cases
○ Two students with reasons for and against.

IDEA 63

SAVE THE CHILDREN

Save the Children is a charity which fights for children in the UK and around the world who suffer from poverty, disease, injustice and violence. It works with them to find lifelong answers to the problems they face.

There is a lot of information about Save the Children (for which the Princess Royal has worked tirelessly as its patron for many years) on its website www.savethe children.org.uk/

Build your assembly around the work of Save the Children (or invite a speaker). The charity will probably be happy to supply materials to help you. In 2006 Save the Children was active in south Lebanon after extensive bombing by Israel, in the Democratic Republic of Congo where children are being drafted into armed forces and in African countries where AIDS is rife, as well as many other areas.

Spend a minute's silence reflecting on how fortunate most of us are in the assembly hall compared with people of our own age elsewhere in the world.

You will need:
○ Notes on Save the Children or a speaker from the charity.

Should animals be painfully used to test perfume, shampoo and cleaning materials to see if they are safe for human beings to use? Probably not, because there are other ways of testing most of these. But what about drugs and treatments to save lives? Without experiments on animals we probably wouldn't have, for instance, insulin for diabetics, dialysis for kidney patients or antibiotics for infections.

Where we stand on the difficult question of using animals for medical reasons is a moral decision. We need to gather information and to think hard and clearly.

Have prepared two mini-dramas presented by students. One is about a very sick child (cancer perhaps) who is cured by chemotherapy. The other shows a group of animal rights activists vandalizing a research laboratory.

You might pose the questions: should any animal be deliberately hurt? If you are opposed to animal experimentation, should you use the drugs which are developed from it? If you are opposed to the 'violence' of experimenting on animals, is it right to use violence to make your protest?

Aim to get the students to consider the issue rationally from a moral point of view. Make sure both sides of the argument are presented equally.

You will need:
o Notes on animal experimentation
o Students with two sketches prepared.

MEDICAL EXPERIMENTATION ON ANIMALS

IDEA 65

STREET CLEANLINESS

Two things make streets dirty and unhygienic: litter such as 'on-the-go' food wrappings and other unwanted items dropped by humans, and excrement deposited by their dogs.

We don't all have dogs, but we all use the streets. Everyone can help reduce litter levels. Have a group of students call out in turn a list of things like putting sweet wrappers in your pocket, putting fast-food packaging in bins, not letting shop assistants put your purchases in unnecessary bags, disposing of chewing gum by wrapping it up and binning it. And, if you do have a dog, train it, carry plastic bags and use the special bins for 'doggy dos'.

Explain that too many of us don't do this. One council, Medway in Kent, says it collects 5,000 tonnes of litter a year from its streets. Multiply that for the whole country and it runs into hundreds of thousands of tonnes. Forty per cent of all street litter is cigarette butts (scope for an anti-smoking plug here, if appropriate).

End by playing part of George Gershwin's *An American in Paris*. It depicts an attractive street scene. Let's aim to make all our streets pleasant places to be.

You will need:
○ Notes on street cleanliness
○ Students with a list
○ A recording of *An American in Paris*.

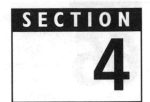

Using music, art and literature

Play the opening of Beethoven's sixth symphony, the *Pastoral*.

Then say something like, 'You have just done something that Beethoven, the composer of that music, could not. You listened to it easily and enjoyed every note.'

Explain that Ludwig van Beethoven's (1770–1827) worsening deafness meant that from his twenties he heard none of his music properly when it was played. He 'heard' it only in his head, and then wrote it down. By the time he was 32 he knew his deafness, probably caused by syphilis, would get worse. He came close to despair.

Much later, in 1824, when Beethoven was totally deaf, he tried to conduct his last symphony but got out of step with the orchestra. It had finished playing and the audience was going wild with enthusiasm, but Beethoven was still conducting. He had to be turned round to see the audience's response. Play a few moments of the choral section of the fourth movement of Beethoven's *Ninth Symphony*.

Deafness is a terrible affliction for anyone, but especially for a musician. Percussionist Evelyn Glennie is profoundly deaf, but she 'hears' the vibration in music. She studied at the Royal Academy of Music in London and won prizes and she is now an international star.

Play a few moments of Evelyn Glennie performing one of the many concertos which have been written for her.

You will need:
○ Recordings of Beethoven's sixth and ninth symphonies
○ An Evelyn Glennie recording.

This is a simple one to celebrate the beauty around us. Read aloud the very short poem 'Pied Beauty' by Gerard Manley Hopkins. Hopkins was a late nineteenth-century British monk and the poem shows his enjoyment of the countryside. William Wordsworth, who lived in the Lake District, came to London nearly a hundred years earlier in 1805 and wrote 'Upon Westminster Bridge', which starts, 'Earth has not anything to show more fair.'

Beauty is everywhere and all around us – suggest local examples, such as baby's faces, cats, part of the school building, fabrics, colours, sounds, smells. Point out that beauty can be in the eye/ear/nose of the beholder. We could all build our own 'beauty list'. It certainly isn't something created by a 'beautician'.

Finish with a beautiful piece of music. It's a personal choice, of course. I'd probably use, with a few words of introduction, 'How Lovely Are Thy Dwellings Fair' from Brahms's *German Requiem* or the second movement of Schubert's *Unfinished Symphony*.

You will need:
○ A copy of 'Pied Beauty'
○ A copy of Wordsworth's poem 'Upon Westminster Bridge'
○ Notes on beauty in the local environment
○ Music to end.

IDEA

68

Read aloud, or get a student to, Enobarbus's description of the Egyptian queen Cleopatra on her ceremonial barge from Shakespeare's play *Antony and Cleopatra* (Act II scene ii). Alternatively you could show a video or DVD clip of the same passage.

Make the point that it is great 'original' dramatic poetry. Then read this, Shakespeare's source material:

> *She disdained to set forward otherwise but to take her barge in the river of Cydnus, the poop whereof was of gold, the sails of purple, and the oars of silver, which kept stroke in rowing after the sound of the music of flutes, howboys, cithems, viols and other such instruments as they played upon the barge. And now for the person herself: she was laid under a pavilion of cloth of gold of tissue, apparelled and attired like the goddess Venus commonly drawn in picture; and hard by her, on either hand of her, pretty fair boys apparelled as painters do set forth god Cupid, with little fans in their hands, with which they fanned wind upon her.*

From *Plutarch*, c. 50–120 AD

So was Shakespeare a plagiarist?

This is an opportunity to talk about plagiarism and school work, acknowledging the fineness of the line between plagiarism and research. Mention copyright law and that it is theft to take someone else's work without permission. (Plutarch had been dead for 1,500 years before Shakespeare plundered him!)

You will need:
○ A copy of *Antony and Cleopatra* or a video/DVD clip
○ The extract from Plutarch
○ Notes on plagiarism today.

This straightforward idea is based on the various interpretations of Psalm 23. Play, read, or have read by students, the following:

- ○ 'The King of Love my Shepherd is' sung by a choir such as King's College, Cambridge or Huddersfield Choral Society
- ○ Psalm 23 from the Authorized Version of the Bible
- ○ the Crimond setting of 'The Lord's My Shepherd'
- ○ Psalm 23 read from a modern version of the Bible
- ○ a recording of 'The Lord's my Shepherd' set to 'Brother James's Air'.

(If there is a school choir or group which could sing one or more of these versions live, then so much the better.)

I find this works with very little comment. You might just want to say that the psalm – one of a set of 150 hymns/poems/prayers from the Bible – is often used at both weddings and funerals. The beautiful words have inspired many musicians and poets.

You will need:
- ○ Two different versions of the written psalm
- ○ Three different recordings of the psalm set to music.

IDEA

70

Read aloud the poem 'We are Seven' by William Wordsworth. The little girl in the poem has accepted quite readily that her brother has died. But for her it isn't an end. He is just in another place and she goes to the churchyard where he's buried to play with him in her imagination. She still regards him as a member of her family.

Show one of the filmed versions of *Macbeth* – the scene in which the Macduff family are killed (Act IV scene ii). The child is wiser than his mother.

Play Danny Kaye singing 'The Emperor's New Clothes', a version of the well-known story from the 1952 film *Hans Christian Andersen*. It is a child who spots that the Emperor has no new clothes and refuses to pretend.

The Bible has an expression 'out of the mouths of babes and sucklings'. Listen to young children. They can sometimes grasp things that adults or older children miss because they can see directly to the heart of something without all the doubts which experience brings.

You will need:

o The poem 'We are Seven'
o A video/DVD of *Macbeth*, in the right place
o A recording of 'The Emperor's New Clothes'.

This is a very simple idea for remembering loved ones or those who are no longer around. Three pieces of music do the work for you.

Play Elton John's 'Candle in the Wind' (the version he performed at the funeral of Diana, Princess of Wales in 1997).

Read aloud 'Remember,' a sonnet by Christina Rossetti. Then play Dido's lament from Henry Purcell's *Dido and Aeneas*. Dido's love is leaving her and sailing away across the sea. She sings this lament in her despair.

It doesn't really need a lot of comment, except perhaps that when we are feeling deeply unhappy words and music can sometimes help. You might also say that even if we have never felt an emotion such as great loss ourselves, art and music can help us to empathize with those who have.

You will need:
o A copy of 'Remember' by Christina Rossetti
o A recording of Dido's lament
o A recording of 'Candle in the Wind'.

Show the assembly a reproduction of Henri Rousseau's *Tiger in a Tropical Storm (surprised)*. The original is in the National Gallery in London. Use a poster, an electronic whiteboard image or show them a plate in a book (if you have to resort to the latter you will have to describe the picture very carefully because it won't be very visible from the back). There's more information and a reproduction of the painting at www.tate.org.uk/modern/exhibitions/rousseau/default.shtm because it featured in Tate Modern's 2006 exhibition *Jungles in Paris*.

Rousseau was a late nineteenth-century Frenchman who fell in love with his imaginary version of the tropics, even though he never left France. He painted a whole series of these very dramatic jungle pictures. If he were alive today Rousseau would undoubtedly be an environmentalist. Tigers are on the brink of extinction. Their numbers declined by 95 per cent during the twentieth century. Using Rousseau as a starting point, build an assembly around the plight of the tiger.

End by reading aloud William Blake's poem 'The Tyger', which starts 'Tyger! Tyger! burning bright'.

You will need:
o A reproduction of Rousseau's painting
o Facts and figures about tigers
o A copy of 'The Tyger'.

This is a way of teaching the students a little more about a famous and familiar piece and its history so that they think about the music and its implications rather than just taking it for granted. It also shows how attitudes to art change. What we hear now is not necessarily what people heard a hundred years ago.

Play the 'big tune' from Elgar's 'Pomp and Circumstance March Number 4' (this is *not* 'Land of Hope and Glory').

English composer Edward Elgar (1857–1934) wrote a series of five marches under the name *Pomp and Circumstance* (the title is a quotation from Shakespeare's *Othello*) because he liked noble-sounding music. Many people find his music very stirring.

The most famous of the series is Number 1. The tune was set to the words 'Land of Hope and Glory', written by A. C. Benson for the coronation of Edward VII in 1902. It quickly became a 'patriotic' piece – a sort of second national anthem. But Elgar, a musician with many German friends and colleagues, was very upset when it was used as a pro-English, anti-German song during World War One.

Today it is always sung and played by orchestra, choir and audience on the last night of the Proms (a series of concerts which runs for two months in London's Royal Albert Hall each summer).

Play first an orchestral version of the big tune from 'Pomp and Circumstance March Number 1' as Elgar originally wrote it. Then play a version with singing or possibly show a video clip of the appropriate moment from the last night of the Proms.

You will need:
o A recording of 'Pomp and Circumstance March Number 4'
o Recordings of 'Pomp and Circumstance March Number 1' (with and without singing)
o Notes on Elgar and the background of 'Land of Hope and Glory'.

IDEA 73

POMP AND CIRCUMSTANCE

IDEA

74

SMALL PEOPLE

Play a recording of Gavroche's song 'Little People' from Act II of *Les Misérables* or use a video/DVD clip from the *Les Misérables* concert given at the Royal Albert Hall. The song says that you shouldn't underestimate people because they are small.

Read aloud the story of David and Goliath from the Bible (1 Samuel 17.38–51). The odds were stacked against the small-framed David because his enemy was a huge man. But David outwitted him.

Mention small people in history such as Horatio Nelson and Toulouse Lautrec, both very successful in their fields. Make your own list. The point is that it is brain and personality which count, not size. Finish by playing the *Les Misérables* number again.

You will need:
○ A recording of *Les Misérables* soundtrack or video/DVD of the concert
○ A Bible
○ A list of successful small people.

Like Idea 73, this is an assembly about music exploration which tells the student a bit more about a piece of music probably familiar to many, although few will know its history. Next time they hear it, some will respond in a different way now that they have this information.

Play a recording of the popular hymn 'Abide with Me'. I would, at this point probably personalize this assembly with an anecdote about my earliest memory of it (habitually sung by my grandmother as she did the housework).

It was written by Henry Francis Lyte (1793–1847) just before his death from tuberculosis (TB). It's a bit melancholy and that may be why it's often used at funerals. The tune was written by William H. Monk in 1861.

'Abide with Me' was the favourite hymn of Mahatma Gandhi and also of King George V. Queen Elizabeth II chose it for her wedding, and so did her father, George VI. In 1927 it was sung for the first time at the F. A. Cup Final before the match. It became a tradition and is now always sung then, along with the National Anthem.

Play the hymn again to end or, if appropriate, display the words and get the assembly to sing it together.

You will need:
○ A recording of 'Abide with Me'
○ The words of 'Abide with Me' and accompaniment if students are to sing it
○ Notes on the hymn's history.

Single class assemblies

These ideas are suitable for occasions when you have to lead an assembly in a classroom, usually with your own class. Ideally these involve the students as much as possible and end with something to unite the group. If there's any way you can change the seating quickly and easily for the assembly it will give the room a different mood.

BENJAMIN ZEPHANIAH

Share a reading (with several student taking part) of a selection of poems by Benjamin Zephaniah, such as 'Talking Turkeys', any of his vegetarian work or some of his angry material about racism in Britain.

Zephaniah's ancestral Jamaican voice (although he was born in Birmingham, UK) is so strong that, ideally, the readings should be by students who can make a good fist of imitating his voice. Hold a class discussion about Zephaniah's words and what he stands for.

You could easily make two separate class assemblies from this – one on vegetarianism/veganism and another on racial equality. There is plenty of information at www.benjaminzephaniah.com/

To involve the whole class, you could finish with a unison reading of one of Zephaniah's raps, led by the pupils who presented the poems at the beginning. Give out photocopied sheets or have the text displayed on the electronic whiteboard.

You will need:
o   A prepared reading of Zephaniah's work
o   Points or questions to trigger discussion
o   The text of a rap to end with.

Tell the class a short anecdote about an occasion when someone was particularly kind to you. I usually use the time when I had a road accident and a woman in a passing car produced a flask of hot tea. I was unhurt but very upset and her kindness really helped.

Divide the class into pairs. Get each pair to take turns to tell each other about either a time when they benefited from someone else's kindness or when they saw someone being kind to someone else. They won't have difficulty thinking of anecdotes, so after about four minutes, 30 or so instances of kindness will have been described.

The point to draw out is that there is a great deal of kindness about and it's a very important part of how human beings relate to each other. It is just a pity that we are led by newspapers and other media not to notice kindness because they feed us a near-exclusive diet of the opposite: abuse, crime, rudeness and other forms of unkindness.

There is an old Native American proverb that you cannot understand a man until you have walked a mile in his moccasins. End with half a minute's silence to think about the implications of that.

You will need:
o A prepared anecdote about kindness.

IDEA 77

KINDNESS

HELPING EACH OTHER

Divide the class into pairs. In each pair one student puts his or her left hand behind his/her back. The other does the same with the right. They have one right and one left hand available between them. Then give each student four paper clips. The task is to make a chain from the paper clips using nothing but the free hand. It is difficult, if not impossible.

Then tell them to do the same task working with their partner, so two hands cooperate although they belong to different people. The task then becomes quite quick and easy. Ask the students what they noticed. They will probably say they had to talk about it and work out the best way.

This is an example of how we can help each other, despite any disadvantages we face. Two can achieve things which one cannot. Ask the class for everyday examples of this – they might mention teamwork in sports and games or working together in projects. You could also mention clubs, interest groups, even trade unions, when you draw the discussion together.

End with a short brainstorming activity about all the ways in which we can help each other both in and out of school.

You will need:
o Paper clips.

Get three students to share a reading aloud of the passage beginning, 'These I have loved' from 'The Great Lover' by Rupert Brooke. Then go round the whole class asking each student in turn to mention something that he or she likes. You, as teacher, take a turn and join in (my own favourites, for instance, include donkeys, bassoons, all shades of mauve, irises, velvet). No one needs to comment. They should just listen to each other's choices.

You can probably go round the group several times. Then draw the exercise together by pointing out what a lot of positive things there are in the world which make people happy and how interesting it is that we all like such different things – yet another aspect of diversity.

End by listening together to a recording of 'My Favourite Things' from *The Sound of Music*.

You will need:
○ Students ready to present from 'The Great Lover'
○ A recording of *The Sound of Music* soundtrack.

MY FAVOURITE THINGS

IDEA

80

INVITE A VISITOR

Working with the pupils, identify well in advance someone who could talk interestingly to the class for about ten minutes. It could be:

o a parent/grandparent or other relation with an unusual job (for example, fire officer, theatre critic or religious leader)
o a teacher or other staff member from elsewhere in the school who has an unusual hobby (for example, windsurfing, wood carving or folk singing)
o someone from the wider school community, such as a doctor, police officer, head of a primary school
o an elderly person with interesting memories of, for example, being evacuated during World War Two.

Pupils, under supervision, could write or email to invite the visitor. Make it clear that the assembly is very short – a ten-minute presentation plus five minutes for questions.

One student should introduce the speaker, another chair the questions and a third thank him/her for coming. Students can also be on hand to greet the speaker and to do the seeing out at the end. There is quite a lot of PSHE and citizenship potential in this exercise.

You will need:
o Carefully briefed students
o Watertight arrangements about times, access and so on made with the visitor.

Before the assembly, ask the students to think about what worries them. Find three class members who are willing to share their worries with the rest of the class and ask them to prepare a three-minute presentation each. You may have to do one yourself as a role model. Worries could be local, quite personal or global. The sort of topics which work well for this are:

○ global warming
○ declining population in the UK
○ taking important exams
○ leaving school
○ overuse of petrol-driven vehicles
○ rising crime rates
○ dumbed-down TV programmes
○ religious extremism
○ the proposed building scheme for the local town centre.

At the end, thank the three participants and make it clear that the purpose of this is to share worries because, 'A worry shared is a worry halved'. End with half a minute's silence to think about what has been said.

If a high number of students come up with worries to share you may find you have the material for more than one class assembly.

You will need:
○ Three students with prepared presentations.

IDEA

81

STUDENT WORRIES

IDEA

82

MINI MUSIC FESTIVAL

Talk to the class about this in advance. Find three volunteers who have pieces of music – preferably a variety – which mean something special to them. In the assembly each student in turn plays his or her music extract to the class. The limit is strictly two minutes' playing time and one minute explaining the piece.

You may have to be one of the three volunteers yourself to role model it. I have used the Beatles' 'Yesterday' because it takes me back to the coffee bar in the college where I trained as a teacher, the opening of Wagner's *Tannhäuser* overture (the beauty of the trombones over the strings reduces me to tears every time) and Edvard Grieg's *Hall of the Mountain King* because it was one of the very first pieces of classical music I got to know when I was at primary school.

Students often get so enthusiastic about this that they all want a turn, in which case you may find you have the content for a whole series of assemblies.

You will need:
○ Three students, each with a piece of music to share.

CLASS ACHIEVEMENTS

What has this class achieved as a group? School trophies for sport, academic work, points gained for newspaper recycling, money raised for a charity? There are many possibilities. Draw from the group as varied a list as possible.

Then move on to individual achievements, both in and out of school, of which the class can be proud. Encourage them to tell the class about each other's achievements which might not otherwise be known about, partly because the achievers don't know how to mention things about themselves. For example, 'Gemma got her 100 metres certificate at the town swimming club last week' or 'Luke has had a letter published in the local paper'.

As the ideas come up record them on an electronic whiteboard or marker board or use post-its. It should prove that 'we' have actually achieved a great deal and we could probably do even more. Try to create some sort of display which can be left up after the assembly for students to look at quietly later.

The purpose of this is to show we should celebrate all kinds of success, not just in academic work, and to try to build a culture in which success is something good, not a cause for sneering at each other.

You will need:
o A way of recording the achievements.

IDEA
84

WHAT'S IN THE NEWS?

Like Ideas 45 and 48 this is a way of using something in the news, but in a class assembly rather than a larger one.

Get the students to bring cuttings from newspapers (or print-outs from Internet news services such as news.bbc.co.uk) about something reported in the last few days focusing on people being especially brave, dignified, enterprising, imaginative or making new discoveries.

Go round the group and get each student to say in one sentence what his or her report is about. For example, 'My cutting is about Mr and Mrs Taylor, parents of Damilola, who behaved with great dignity when their son's killers were convicted' (August 2006).

The purpose of this, and the point to make as you draw it together at the end, is that there is a great deal of positive news in the world, even if it is buried within bad news. If you ask students to come not only with their cuttings but also with their sentences prepared it is also, incidentally, a useful exercise in summary. Put all the cuttings on a noticeboard for students to look at later.

You will need:
○ Students prepared with cuttings and summaries.

This works in the same way as Idea 82, but this time using poems instead of music. Talk to the class about this in advance and find three volunteers who have poems – preferably a variety – which mean something special to them. They need to be short poems, such as a sonnet, or an extract from something longer.

In the assembly, each student reads aloud his or her poem to the class. The limit is strictly two minutes' reading time and one minute explaining the piece.

You may have take part yourself in order to demonstrate the exercise. I have successfully used 'The Zebras' by Roy Campbell, the opening of the 'Lady of Shallot' by Tennyson and various Shakepeare sonnets.

If many students want a turn you may find that this provides the material for more than one class assembly.

You will need:
o Three students, each with a poem to share.

MINI POETRY FESTIVAL

Class-led assemblies

In many schools each class plans and leads an assembly on a rota basis so that your turn comes round once every couple of terms. It's a good opportunity for a form teacher to work with his or her students on a collaborative project. Of course, the ideas should, and will, come from the students, but they may need guidance and/or containment. These are possible starting points which would work for any age group in a secondary school or for a mixed-age tutor group. Encourage the involvement of as many class members as possible.

HELPING OTHERS

The students in the class devise in advance a mini-play showing different ways of helping others – in the family, in school, in the local neighbourhood, through a charity, in the developing world through a school project or in a 'gap' year, for example.

It would also be possible to get several different groups of four or five students each to work out a short sketch on a theme. These could then be presented to the assembly as a series.

It then needs three or four 'lead' students to draw the assembly together by pointing out that Jesus Christ, Mohammed, Buddha and most other great religious leaders advocated human beings helping one another. Short quotes from their teachings might be appropriate.

A piece of music always goes down well as a finishing point. Challenge the students by encouraging them to find an appropriate piece.

You will need:
○ Prepared student play(s)
○ Lead students with explanations, quotes, etc.
○ Music and a way of playing it.

One way of presenting this topic would be for a small group of students to read aloud short extracts from novels, news, reports and poems which relate to fairness or lack of it. Ideally you need about six.

Get the students to comb newspapers and Internet news sites and to think about books and poems they have read independently or in English lessons to find examples. 'Classic' possibilities include the moment in *Jane Eyre* when the young Jane is accused by Mr Brocklehurst of subversiveness, and almost any paragraph from *Animal Farm*. Wendy Cope's poem 'Tich Miller' would work too. The students will have their own ideas. Aim for a good range.

After the readings one student could define fairness and explain why it is desirable, but not always possible, and how we should always aim for it. They could choose to end with a half-minute's silence to think about the victims of unfairness.

You will need:
o Students with suitable readings
o One student to sum up.

IDEA
88

SAYING NO

There are many ways of presenting this topic. If your group wants to tackle it but can't think how, here is one possibility. This is a way of making the students aware that they should refuse drugs, excessive alcohol and unwanted sexual advances, and it gives them some idea of how they might do this.

Get three pairs of students to role-play three situations. One student does and says everything he or she can think of to persuade the other to accept the drugs, drink or sexual intimacy. The second student says nothing except the word 'no'. (If you stage these as if the pair was at a party, the rest of the tutor group can be the other guests.)

This is known as the gramophone record technique. The refuser is like an old-fashioned LP which has got stuck. He or she is so busy saying 'no' that he/she isn't really listening to the persuader and so is not persuaded. The persuader on the other hand gets bored and irritated, gives up and goes off to try someone else. So it works!

After the audience has watched the three role-played examples, one or two students could sum up and explain (as above) why it's a successful technique. A few stark statistics about the number of teenagers in trouble because of drugs, drink or underage pregnancy, sexually transmitted diseases and so on would fit well too. But, as always, remember this assembly belongs to the students and they will have their own ideas.

You will need:
o Six students with prepared, paired role-plays
o One or two students to sum up.

This is the assembly all Key Stage 3 classes love because it gives them an excuse to don football scarves and hats and pretend to be rival groups of fans fighting. They probably won't need much prompting from you – in fact, if you're not careful, all class-led assemblies tend to become this one! So you need to sort out some ground rules. Get them to think clearly about what point of good behaviour they are trying to encourage –probably that we should be sportsmanlike, respect the other side, take the may-the-best-team-win view and behave without aggression at matches.

One possibility is to get them to do two plays – one which shows bad behaviour and then a rerun showing the opposite behaviour. Smiles and friendly greetings often disarm aggression, so the second version could show that. Another option is to make one a tennis match. Spectators tend to be orderly at tennis matches and they are quite fun to act because the whole class can be the audience watching the course of an imaginary ball.

A good opening to this assembly is some sporty music such as 'Football Crazy', 'Ere we go' or 'Abide with Me'. But the students must choose. They may well know some suitable sports-related piece which is new to you (and me).

Someone from the class should sum up at the end and explain why good behaviour at sports events should be the rule.

You will need:
o Mini-plays prepared by the class
o A student to sum up
o Some suitable music.

BEING A SPORTING SPECTATOR

IDEA 90

Shoplifting is theft and shoplifters are thieves. It isn't a game and most shops now routinely prosecute shoplifters. It can get offenders a criminal record. The purpose of this assembly is to show how serious it is.

Working well in advance of the assembly, get the class or a small group to write a monologue. The speaker is a convicted, unhappy shoplifter. He or she describes what she/he did and why, being caught, how it felt and so on. Then, in the assembly, one student performs the monologue (make it absolutely clear that is a piece of drama. It isn't the student speaking about personal experience). Then build the rest of the assembly around other students in the class questioning the 'shoplifter' or making constructive comments.

There might also be scope here to invite a local shopkeeper or manager, store detective, police officer or magistrate to add a few words about shoplifting if that is how the students would like to organize it.

You will need:
o A student monologue
o Other students ready to make a contribution
o An outside speaker (optional).

FAVOURITE BOOKS

Get three or four students to talk for two minutes each about a book they have read recently which they would like to recommend to the assembly. You will need to vet the choices for appropriateness, variety and the avoidance of repetition.

Suggest that they have a copy of the book there to hold up so that the audience can see the cover. Make the students responsible for liaising with the school librarian well in advance to check that she or he has copies of the featured books in stock in case there is a run on these titles after the assembly.

The assembly ends with the whole class, each with a book, pretending to be totally absorbed in it for half a minute or so. This will reinforce the value of silent reading and involve the entire group.

You will need:
o Students carefully prepared to 'sell' their books
o Each class member with a book.

THE PRODIGAL SON

Some time before the assembly get the students to read – or read with them and discuss – the Christian parable of the prodigal son (St Luke 15.11–32).

Using as large a cast as they wish, the students then devise a play version of the story, modernizing it as they wish. So the sons can be daughters, looking after the pigs could be cleaning the lavatories, killing the fatted calf could be getting from the freezer something extra good saved for a special occasion and so on. If you give them a free rein the students will come up with lots of ideas.

In the assembly get one student, or a small group of students, to read aloud the original Bible story. Point out that it is about forgiveness and then say something like 'Forgiveness is still important today. Here is our version of the story.'

You will need:
o A Bible
o A student to read the story and introduce the play
o A prepared mini-play based on the prodigal son story.

Girls and women are supposed to find it easier to ask for help than boys and men.

Prepare two pairs of funny sketches to expose the stereotype. One could be a couple in a car who are lost. She won't ask the way but eventually he does. Then replay it with the roles reversed. The second could be a boy and a girl doing homework together. They get stuck. One of them asks for help to the disapproval of the other. Then replay it with the roles reversed.

Then one student, or a small group, addresses the assembly directly, making the points that a) it isn't a sign of weakness to ask for help, b) if you need help the simplest thing is to ask someone, c) asking for help is actually a sign of strength and confidence, d) how prepared are we to help if someone asks us?

Each member of the class could have a one-phrase example of specific circumstances in which you need to ask for help. They could call them out in a sequence to round off the assembly. This would also be a way of involving the whole class. The list could go something like: Ask for help when . . . you've left your pen at home . . . you're stuck in maths . . . you can't get the top off your water bottle . . . your phone has run out of charge . . . you don't know the name of a teacher you need to speak to.

You will need:
- ○ Student sketches prepared
- ○ Student(s) to draw points together
- ○ Every student in the class ready with an example of when you need help.

ASKING FOR HELP

IDEA 94

Tolerance is a tricky, two-edged word. It is a good and desirable quality when it's applied to, say, relations between people of different cultures or backgrounds. It is a very negative, weak concept when it is applied to passive tolerance of, for example, crime or gang warfare. Then there's zero tolerance, which isn't the same as intolerance. Hold a pre-assembly session in which the class considers and discusses the connotations of tolerance.

The thrust of the assembly is then drawing attention to the things that we should tolerate, such as the customs of friends and neighbours different from our own, or should not tolerate, such as bullying.

The students need to devise a way of presenting this division. One possibility is prepared role-plays to highlight different sorts of tolerance and intolerance. Another would be for a group of students to mount a joint presentation about all the different aspects of tolerance. (A good example might be the zero tolerance of street crime established by Rudy Giuliani, Mayor of New York from 1993–2001. The city is now much safer for ordinary people than it used to be.)

A rounding-off activity could be to divide the class into two halves. One half takes it in turn to call out things like racism, street litter, using a wheelchair which can get in other people's way, very loud music at 2 am. The other half calls out yes or no. Then they change over.

You will need:
○ Students ready to present the tolerance theme in whatever way the group decides
○ The whole class ready to call out actions and attitudes to tolerate or not (optional).

The more multicultural diversity there is in the class the better this will work. Get as many pupils in the class as possible – preferably all of them – to make a very short statement about a foodstuff or dish from their own culture. For example, a pupil from a Jamaican background might say something like, 'One of my favourite Jamaican dishes is rice and peas. The peas are really red kidney beans cooked in a rich spicy sauce. It's delicious and vegetarian too!'

Or a pupil from Latvia could say, 'From Latvia I love piragi which are meat, bacon and onion pasties. My mum and dad use to have them when they were children in Riga. Now they make them to remind themselves of home, and they're really good!'

Really this is just a simple way of celebrating diversity. Make sure that children whose ancestors have always lived in Britain are included, with traditions like fish and chips and Yorkshire pudding.

If there are 30 in the class it should be possible to come up with 30 dishes and ensure that everyone leaves assembly feeling hungry! A short silence to think about people all over the world who are starving is a good way of ending.

You will need:
○ Lots of students with very brief presentations on favourite dishes.

Instant fixes

There will almost certainly be times when you have to take an assembly at no notice, perhaps because a colleague is unexpectedly absent or because of some other last-minute crisis. These are simple ideas which need no wordy preparation or complicated props.

Tell the students about a place which you know well or have visited and which is special to you – somewhere you recall from childhood or a place where you had memorable holidays, met someone significant, ran your only marathon, or whatever. Beauty is in the eye of the beholder. The place may not be rationally beautiful, but it is just very important to you. Everyone has places like that.

I have done this successfully with:

○ Hamworthy beach in a scruffy corner of Poole harbour. I spent many happy childhood bucket-and-spade holidays there with the extended family. It still has to be visited, as a pilgrimage, when I'm in the area.
○ Cragside, a Victorian house in Northumberland belonging to The National Trust. I first went there when my children were small and have been back many times. It is rugged, romantic and wonderful.
○ Chichester, the city in Sussex where I trained as a teacher and where I got to know my husband.

If you put your heart into explaining why the place is special, with lots of corroborative detail, this can work very well. There is something spiritual about places with memories.

Talk about an interesting relation or friend of yours from the present or the past. It could be someone who won a bravery award, faced illness with exceptional courage or originality, is/was one of life's eccentrics, bore ten children, writes books, owns an unusual animal . . . Most of us are not short of material when we start to think in assembly mode about the people we know or have known.

Make it clear that this is personal. Give it your all in the telling and they will probably hang on your every word.

AN INTERESTING PERSON

IDEA 98

AN UNUSUAL EVENT

Tell a personal anecdote. I cannot, of course, write these for you, but my own stock includes:

o The night when I was feeding my firstborn at 2 am and I heard a noise outside the front door. Was it something or someone real or . . . ?

o The time when, aged 19, I sang a solo at a staff party at Buckingham Palace attended by the Queen, Prince Philip and . . . , but this is not the place for name dropping!

o The occasion when I was visiting a very small, quiet, World War One trench museum in Belgium and was escorted (shown?) round by a tabby cat.

It shouldn't be difficult to pull something quirky out of your own experience – then just tell it as it happened.

Keep an anthology and a book of five-minute stories handy. Then, in an emergency, all you have to do is quickly choose one you have not used for two or three years and read it aloud as animatedly and with as much eye contact as you can.

Old Testament stories are good for this too. Stories such as Joseph, Daniel in the Lions' Den and Noah's Flood have stood the test of time and still go down well. David Kossoff's retellings are especially attractive in *Old and New: Bible Stories Retold*, for example.

A POEM OR STORY

A SIGNIFICANT OBJECT

Look at your desk or in your handbag or car. Find an object which is special to you. It could be, for example, a:

o   special pen
o   paper weight
o   book
o   photograph
o   key fob
o   piece of jewellery
o   CD.

Tell the students its story – where you got it from, what you associate it with and why it is important to you.

I once did a surprisingly successful assembly on this basis. Its starting point was my grandfather's watch chain which I use as a necklace and happened to be wearing that day. He survived a serious injury from a sniper's bullet in France in 1915. He always said the wound saved his life because he was transported home. Then, while he was recovering in Brighton from his injuries and many operations, he met the girl who became my grandmother. If he hadn't, I wouldn't be here and someone else would have been taking this assembly, wearing this necklace and writing this book.

MORE DATES

You could create more date-specific assemblies by using:

○ No Smoking Day – mid-March
○ Father's Day – third Sunday in June
○ Grandparents' Day – fourth Saturday in September
○ St Matthew's Day – 21 September
○ National Poetry Day – early October
○ United Nations Day – 24 October
○ All Saints' Day – 1 November

MORE BEHAVIOUR TOPICS

In addition to the ones suggested in Section 3, here are some more possible starting points for behaviour-focused assemblies:

○ thoughtfulness
○ gentleness
○ respect for shop staff
○ behaviour in the street
○ conscientious attitude to school work

More of these will crop up during the school year. There are times when a behaviour matter needs to be discussed because of something which has happened, or a trend which has developed. It's worth keeping your own cumulative list.

MORE ISSUES

As well as the suggestions in Section 4, there are many other issues which would make assembly topics. For example:

○ live export of food animals
○ noise pollution
○ light pollution
○ water shortage.

Add to this list as ideas occur to you and issues move in and out of the news.

POEMS FOR ASSEMBLIES

A number of specific poems have already been mentioned in this book but there are plenty more which could make a starting point for an assembly. Look in:

- ○ *The Oxford Book of Christmas Poems* ed. Michael Harrison and Christopher Stuart Clark
- ○ *The New Dragon Book of Verse* ed. Michael Harrison and Christopher Stuart-Clark
- ○ *The Rattlebag* ed. Seamus Heaney and Ted Hughes
- ○ *A Poem a Day* chosen by Adrian Mitchell
- ○ www.poetry-online.org

OTHER RESOURCES FOR GOOD ASSEMBLIES

- ○ *The Secondary Assembly File* (a pfp subscription publication – a new batch of assemblies arrives three times a year). See www.pfp-publishing.com
- ○ *Challenges for Living: Fifty Assemblies for Secondary Schools* by Ian Stuart, Religious and Moral Education Press
- ○ *Just think about that! Outlines for Secondary Assemblies* by Phil Wason, Scripture Union Publishing
- ○ *Assemble Together: sixty topical assemblies for secondary schools* by Tony Castle, Kevin Mayhew Ltd
- ○ www.assemblies.org.uk
- ○ www.assemblingcitizens.co.uk
- ○ *One Voice Please: Tales of Truth and Trickery* by Sam McBratney and illustrated by Russell Ayto was published by Walker Books in 2005. It contains pithy retellings of stories from many periods and countries – most of them thought-provoking and with good lessons to be drawn out. They come from Aesop, the Bible, legend, myth, folk culture and many other sources. Most are an ideal length for reading aloud in a secondary school assembly.